# Blender for Video Production Quick Start Guide

Create high quality videos for YouTube and other social media platforms with Blender

**Allan Brito**

BIRMINGHAM - MUMBAI

# Blender for Video Production Quick Start Guide

**Commissioning Editor:** Amarabha Banerjee
**Acquisition Editor:** Reshma Raman
**Content Development Editor:** Roshan Kumar
**Technical Editor:** Niral Almeida
**Copy Editor:** Safis Editing
**Project Coordinator:** Hardik Bhinde
**Proofreader:** Safis Editing
**Indexer:** Priyanka Dhadke
**Graphics:** Alishon Mendonsa
**Production Coordinator:** Nilesh Mohite

First published: November 2018

Production reference: 1291118

Published by Packt Publishing Ltd.
Livery Place
35 Livery Street
Birmingham
B3 2PB, UK.

ISBN 978-1-78980-495-9

www.packtpub.com

*For my nephews, Mateus and Daniel. The joy of family!*

*– Allan Brito*

`mapt.io`

Mapt is an online digital library that gives you full access to over 5,000 books and videos, as well as industry leading tools to help you plan your personal development and advance your career. For more information, please visit our website.

## Why subscribe?

- Spend less time learning and more time coding with practical eBooks and Videos from over 4,000 industry professionals

- Improve your learning with Skill Plans built especially for you

- Get a free eBook or video every month

- Mapt is fully searchable

- Copy and paste, print, and bookmark content

## Packt.com

Did you know that Packt offers eBook versions of every book published, with PDF and ePub files available? You can upgrade to the eBook version at `www.packt.com` and as a print book customer, you are entitled to a discount on the eBook copy. Get in touch with us at `customercare@packtpub.com` for more details.

At `www.packt.com`, you can also read a collection of free technical articles, sign up for a range of free newsletters, and receive exclusive discounts and offers on Packt books and eBooks.

# Contributors

## About the author

**Allan Brito** is an architect with a strong background in the use of technology in all phases of project development. His friends used to say that he swapped bricks for pixels.

Besides working in the architecture business, he also has more than 10 years of experience as a college teacher, helping students to create animations, 3D games, and mobile apps.

In the academic field, he was in charge of the e-learning department of one of the largest colleges in Brazil for almost eight years, using technologies such as interactive 3D content, games, and virtual reality as learning tools.

Blender is one of the essential tools in his workflow, and he has used it every day since the days of version 2.35 in 2005.

# About the reviewer

**Fernando Castilhos Melo** lives in Toronto, Canada, and works as a software engineer. Since 2009, he has used his spare time to work on 3D modeling using Blender. He has lectured on Blender and 3D modeling at several Brazilian free/open source software events.

Fernando holds a degree in computer science from UCS (Universidade de Caxias do Sul, Brazil), and this is the fourth Blender book that he has worked on. The other ones were *Blender Cycles: Lighting and Rendering Cookbook*, in 2013; *Blender 3D by Example*, in 2015; and *Blender 3D Printing by Example*, in 2017.

Moreover, he has also developed an integration between Blender and Kinect named *Kinected Blender* in order to generate 3D animations using body movements captured from Kinect.

> *I would like to send a big thank you to the following people:*
> *– My wife, Mauren, for all the support she gave me during this reviewing process*
> *– My parents, Eloir and Miriam, for encouraging me*
> *– My dog, Polly, for being (literally) at my side all the time during this review*
> *– All my friends, for giving me the confidence to carry out this work*

# Packt is searching for authors like you

If you're interested in becoming an author for Packt, please visit `authors.packtpub.com` and apply today. We have worked with thousands of developers and tech professionals, just like you, to help them share their insight with the global tech community. You can make a general application, apply for a specific hot topic that we are recruiting an author for, or submit your own idea.

# Table of Contents

# Preface

How can software with a focus on 3D animation and modeling help with video production projects? Blender is an outstanding tool for content creation and has several hidden tools for artists willing to invest some time in learning the software.

The software now even has an integrated game engine for creating interactive 3D content.

Among all those hidden features of Blender, you will find a non-linear video editor. The primary use of that editor is to help artists with animation production, but since it can manipulate video and audio data, you can extend the application to include much more than just animation.

Using the Video Sequencer Editor in Blender alongside the Movie Clip Editor, you can create full-featured videos and projects. Do you have some footage that you've captured with your smartphone or standalone camera? Blender can help you improve that material by means of effects, audio, and more.

With the release of Blender 2.8, the software is gaining a revamped user interface and some improvements to existing tools, such as Eevee, that will enhance the way we work with Blender.

This book uses an early version of Blender 2.8 as a basis for all chapters, but you won't find any significant problems following the content in future releases.

## Who this book is for

This book is aimed at anyone trying to produce content based on video for platforms such as YouTube. Those artists will need software to cut and edit video footage or make small intro clips, animations, or info graphics for their videos.

## What this book covers

Chapter 1, *Blender as a Video Editor for YouTube*, covers how to find and activate the video production options and also locate the Blender Video Sequencer. You will also learn about video standards and how to prepare Blender to use media footage.

Chapter 2, *Editing and Cutting Video Footage in Blender,* covers how to use Blender tools to cut, edit, and reorder video footage. You will also learn how to use tools to mark your video and remove blank spaces from a project.

Chapter 3, *Using Properties to Enhance Video,* covers how to use some of the most critical options from the properties of your Sequencer, such as reversing a video, adding modifiers, and updating the source file of a strip.

Chapter 4, *Animated Properties for Video Effects,* covers how to create and manage keyframes and include an animated watermark in a video.

Chapter 5, *Creating Intro Videos for YouTube with Text and Motion Graphics,* covers how to use some of the 3D tools in Blender to emulate bi-dimensional animation editor with an orthographic camera. You will also learn how to use multiple scenes in the Sequencer.

Chapter 6, *Using Videos as Textures for 3D Compositions,* covers how to create a 3D composition using multiple objects and videos as textures. You will also learn how to create animation loops with videos and synchronize multiple objects for animation.

Chapter 7, *Adding Sound and Voiceover for YouTube,* covers how to edit audio files by using the same tools used for video footage. You will also learn how to protect audio tracks that are already in sync and how to apply animation to create dynamic effects as well.

Chapter 8, *Aligning 3D Content with Video Using Virtual Cameras,* covers how tracking works in Blender and how to use tracking marks to produce your videos. You will also learn how to add markers to existing footage.

Chapter 9, *Exporting Video for YouTube,* covers how to set up Blender to render a project with all the recommended settings from YouTube using the render properties.

# To get the most out of this book

To fully enjoy Blender and all the capabilities of advanced real-time graphics, you should install all necessary drivers and updated software for your graphics card. For the first four chapters, the book uses Blender 2.80 alpha 2 as a basis, while later chapters use Blender 2.80 beta. You will find minor changes in the UI between both versions, but you probably won't encounter any problems following the book with all future versions of Blender 2.8x.

# Download the color images

We also provide a PDF file that has color images of the screenshots/diagrams used in this book. You can download it here:
`http://www.packtpub.com/sites/default/files/downloads/9781789804959_ColorImages.pdf.`

# Code in action

Visit the following link to check out videos of the code being run:

`http://bit.ly/2SkIAxQ`

# Conventions used

There are a number of text conventions used throughout this book.

`CodeInText`: Indicates code words in text, database table names, folder names, filenames, file extensions, pathnames, dummy URLs, user input, and Twitter handles. Here is an example: "For instance, if you have a video file using 60 FPS and Blender is set to use 24 FPS, your playback speed will be slower than the video."

**Bold**: Indicates a new term, an important word, or words that you see on screen. For example, words in menus or dialog boxes appear in the text like this. Here is an example: "To achieve that, you must use an option from the **File** menu in the **External Data** group."

 Warnings or important notes appear like this.

 Tips and tricks appear like this.

# Get in touch

Feedback from our readers is always welcome.

**General feedback**: If you have questions about any aspect of this book, mention the book title in the subject of your message and email us at `customercare@packtpub.com`.

**Errata**: Although we have taken every care to ensure the accuracy of our content, mistakes do happen. If you have found a mistake in this book, we would be grateful if you would report this to us. Please visit www.packt.com/submit-errata, selecting your book, clicking on the Errata Submission Form link, and entering the details.

**Piracy**: If you come across any illegal copies of our works in any form on the internet, we would be grateful if you would provide us with the location address or website name. Please contact us at copyright@packt.com with a link to the material.

**If you are interested in becoming an author**: If there is a topic that you have expertise in, and you are interested in either writing or contributing to a book, please visit authors.packtpub.com.

# Reviews

Please leave a review. Once you have read and used this book, why not leave a review on the site that you purchased it from? Potential readers can then see and use your unbiased opinion to make purchase decisions, we at Packt can understand what you think about our products, and our authors can see your feedback on their book. Thank you!

For more information about Packt, please visit packt.com.

# Blender as a Video Editor for YouTube
# 1

Blender is a fantastic tool for 3D content creation, but it also has some impressive tools related to video production. In the following chapter, you will learn how to find and activate the video production options and also locate the Blender **Video Sequencer**.

With the **Sequencer**, you have a fully functional non-linear video editing space that you can use to either cut and edit a series of footage or take 3D content and make an animation.

You will also learn about video standards and how to prepare Blender to use media footage. Here is what you will learn:

- How to use workspaces in Blender
- How to navigate the **Video Sequencer**
- How to make a video preview
- How to manipulate video strips
- How to prepare footage for import
- How to embed footage to Blender projects

That's just the start! In the following chapters, you will also apply animation and motion graphics techniques to produce all types of video-related material for your professional or personal use.

## Technical requirements

You will be required to have Blender 2.80 installed to follow this procedure. Even if you have a later version of Blender, the described example should work with no significant problems.

The media files of this chapter can be found on GitHub:
`https://github.com/PacktPublishing/Blender-for-Video-Production-Quick-Start-Guide/tree/master/Chapter01`
Check out the following video to see the procedures in action:
`http://bit.ly/2DNPPKm`

# Using Blender as a video editor

The first time you open Blender, you will see a user interface with lots of tools and buttons and a big area to create 3D content (*Figure 1.1*). One of the primary goals of Blender is to make 3D content for animation, effects, and other types of productions. How is it possible to edit video in Blender? Take a look at the following screenshot:

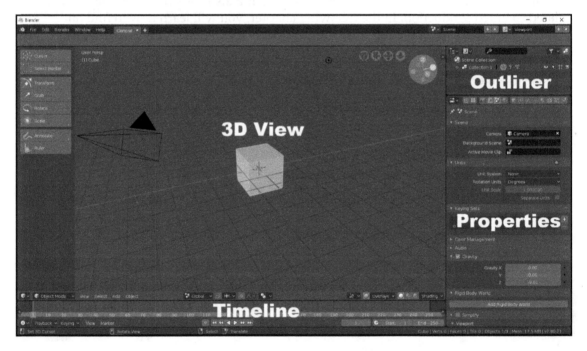

Figure 1.1: Blender default interface

Besides having all those tools for 3D content creation, Blender will also feature a lot more options. One of those options is a video editor inside the software. Unlike many competitors in 3D content creation, Blender's developers wanted to create a tool that could handle all aspects of media production.

If you have an idea that requires 3D content creation that will result in a video file, you can create that in Blender. Better yet, you will be able to get additional footage and blend it with your 3D content.

 In the past, Blender even had an integrated game engine for interactive 3D creation.

One crucial aspect of the Blender user interface that you will notice is that you can change and manipulate almost all aspects related to windows. Look at *Figure 1.1*, and you will see divisions at the interface. Each division might assume a unique function, depending on what you want to do with the software.

The main windows available in the default user interface are the following:

- **3D View**: The sizeable 3D space with a tray cube that will allow you to add and manipulate such content
- **Timeline**: At the bottom of your **3D View** you will see a horizontal window showing options to play back and set animation
- **Properties**: On the right-hand side, you have a tall vertical window called **Properties**, where you will get options to render and change lots of options regarding a scene
- **Outliner**: Finally, we will also find a small window in the upper-right corner with a word, **Collection 1**, where you can organize 3D content in your scene

Which one of these will be the best option for video editing? None of them. We have to use another window that is not part of the default user interface.

# The Blender Video Sequencer and workspaces

If you want to edit video footage in Blender, you need a specific window to manipulate and handle that type of data. You can swap the window type in Blender for an other depending on your project. To change your window type, you can use the small selector available on the left-hand side of each division, as shown in *Figure 1.2*:

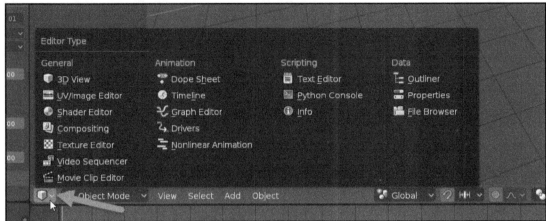

Figure 1.2: Window selector

To edit and manipulate video, we must use a window called **Video Sequencer** (*Figure 1.3*). Using a large window space like the one with our **3D View** will give you plenty of room to work with video editing:

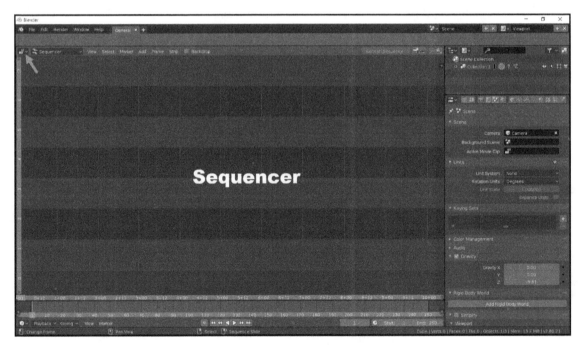

Figure 1.3: Video Sequencer

Once you open the video editor, you will see that such a window has a lot of horizontal spaces. Each of those parallel spaces is a channel, which works like layers. You can stack video footage on top of each other to create a composition.

The footage on channel zero will be at the bottom of the pile, and anything placed at higher channels will be at the top.

We will import and manipulate video and audio inside those channels for any project related to video production.

## Previewing our video project

The Video Sequencer is a great tool to edit and manipulate video footage, but you will quickly notice that it doesn't have any particular area showing a preview of what you have in your project. We can enable a split view of our sequencer with a preview area to help us see the final result.

In the upper-left corner of your **Video Sequencer**, you will find a button for the **View Type** that will be set to Sequencer by default. If you change the button to **Sequencer/Preview**, you will enable the preview window in your **Sequencer** as shown (*Figure 1.4*):

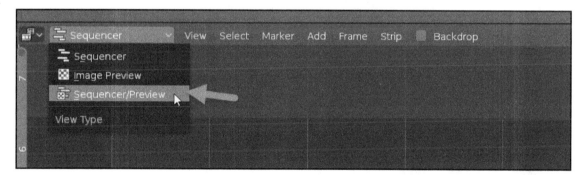

Figure 1.4: Video preview

Once you activate the preview, you will be able to see all video footage at the small top division. That is not a new window, but a divided area of your **Sequencer**.

 After you enable the video preview space, you might experience performance issues on your computer. To have a fluid preview in real time, you must use a powerful computer that can handle massive video editing processing. The purpose of that window is to give you an idea about the visuals of your video composition.

# Workspace for video and YouTube

Having a window like a Video Sequencer is excellent for video production, but wouldn't it be better to have a full interface optimized for video? In Blender, you will find something called workspaces, a user interface layout that has all windows and options for a given task.

You will find the workspaces selector at the top of your user interface (*Figure 1.5*). Click on the + icon to open all options related to workspaces:

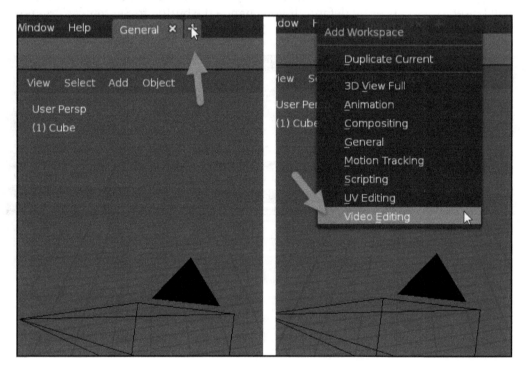

Figure 1.5: Workspace selector

By default, you will have a generic workspace called **General** whenever you start Blender, but we can create many more. From the workspace selector, you can choose different types of user interface arrangements. From that list, you will find the **Video Editing** option.

If you choose that workspace, you will see a complete change to the interface (*Figure 1.6*):

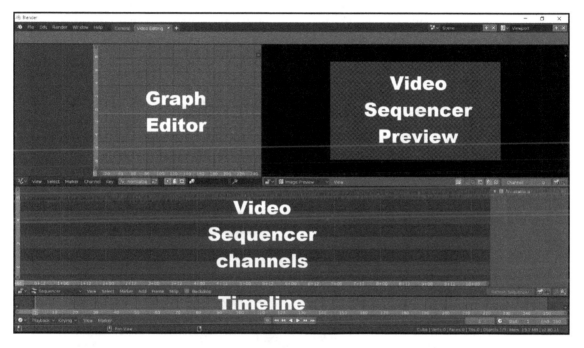

Figure 1.6: Video editing workspace

You still have four windows in the interface, but now with the following layout:

- **Graph Editor**: The upper-left corner has a graph editor to change and manipulate animation data.
- **Video Sequencer Preview**: Still at the top, but on the right hand side, you will find a **Video Sequencer** set to preview only. Look at the **View Type** option, and you will see the **Image Preview** option.
- **Video Sequencer Channels**: In the middle of your screen, we will get a Video Sequencer with the channels, and the **Properties** tab opened.
- **Timeline**: From the default interface, we have the **Timeline** window.

At the top of your screen, you can see the new workspace as a tab. Whenever you need to use the default interface, click on the **General** option and you go back to the default arrangement. To close a workspace tab, you can press the **X** icon on the right hand side of your workspace name.

 A workspace is just an interface arrangement, and you can create as many as you want. You won't lose any data from a workspace that you close.

# Importing video footage to Blender

Having a tool to edit and cut video is an excellent resource for Blender, but how can we import video footage to Blender? There are two ways to import or add media to the **Video Sequencer**. The first one is with the **Add** menu, where you can click at the option and choose from several alternatives (*Figure 1.7*):

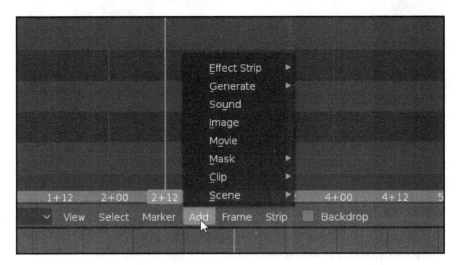

Figure 1.7: Add menu

As you can see from the screenshot, we have an option to add the following:

- **Movie**: Using this option will import a video file to the **Sequencer**.
- **Image**: If you have to work with images, use this option. It will import either a single file or a sequence of images.
- **Sound**: For music and sound, you must use this option.

The **Add** menu has a shortcut for quick access in the **Video Sequencer**. If you press the *Shift + A* keys when your mouse cursor is anywhere, the **Video Sequencer** window will show a pop-up menu with the same options.

Why does the cursor position matter? Blender has a lot of shortcuts that will save you time on different tasks. Since some shortcuts work in a unique way for specific windows, you must tell the software where you want to use a shortcut.

For instance, if you press the *Shift + A* keys with the cursor over the **Timeline** window, nothing will happen. Why? Because in some windows you can't create any objects. If you press the *Shift + A* key with the cursor over a **3D View** window, you will be able to create 3D geometry and not import video footage.

Blender calls the window where your cursor is at the moment the active window. All shortcuts will trigger the action in the active window.

When you press a shortcut and you don't have the expected behavior, look for your cursor.

As you will see when working with Blender, most shortcuts will trigger the same type of action, but for different data types. For instance, selection shortcuts will help you with video editing and also creating 3D Models.

Once you hit the **Movie** option in the menu, you will see a big window in Blender asking you to locate the video file. On the left-hand side of your screen, you will see some options that you might want to review before importing (*Figure 1.8*):

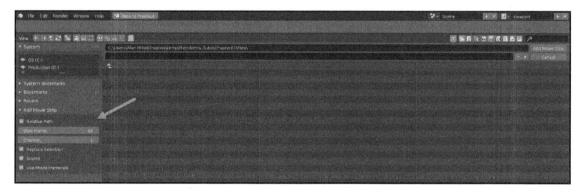

Figure 1.8: Video import options

From top to bottom, here are the options:

- **Relative Path**: Since a movie file is an external resource for Blender, it will need a path to locate the file. The recommendation here is to save your Blender project in a folder and copy all media files there for consistency. If you leave this option enabled, Blender will try to make a relative path to the video file.
- **Start Frame**: The place in your timeline where Blender will place the video file.
- **Replace Selection**: If you have an existing video strip selected in your **Sequencer**, Blender will replace that video with the selected file.
- **Sound**: Do you need the audio from your video? If you want the video and no sound, disable this option.
- **Use Movie Framerate**: Here is an important option! You will have to match the frame rate of your video to Blender's timeline. Otherwise, you might have problems with the playback. By marking this option, Blender will try to make the adjustments for you.

Some of those options need your attention before you import anything to Blender, such as the suggestion to save your Blender file in a folder and copy all the media you will use to that same place to keep relative paths.

Once you get media in the **Sequencer**, you can press the *Shift* + Space bar button to play back any content. If you press the same keys again, it will pause the playback.

# Matching video footage frame rate

Before you start any project related to video in Blender, you should take a look at your video source technical details, to match them in Blender. One of the aspects that you need to identify is the frame rate.

The frame rate is the speed in which all still frames from a video will play. Nowadays, you will find several different types of frame rates for a video—24, 30, 48, and 60 are the most used.

To avoid any potential problems, you must match the frame rate of your video sources to Blender's internal frame rate. For instance, if making a video with your smartphone using 30 FPS, which is the abbreviation for **Frames Per Second**, you must change Blender settings to match.

In Blender, you must go to the **Render** Tab in your **Properties** window (*Figure 1.9*). Look at the **Frame Rate** setting and change it to a value matching your video footage:

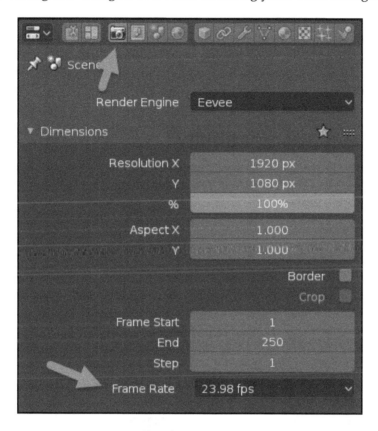

Figure 1.9: Frame rate settings

Using the **General** workspace will give you quick access to that window.

 You can create as many workspaces as you want to keep access to information and properties across Blender windows. Even if you open a **Video Editing** workspace, it would be a great idea to keep the **General** tab available.

What happens if you don't match the frame rate? If you forget to match the value, you will experience playback issues related to speed. For instance, if you have a video file using 60 FPS and Blender is set to use 24 FPS, your playback speed will be slower than the video.

As a result, you will see a slow-motion version of your footage. The opposite also applies, where you might have video footage in 24 FPS and using anything higher will speed up the video playback.

On the other hand, you might want to use Blender to create original content for a video such as an infographic or animation. For the cases where you don't have video footage to work, it is essential to set a frame rate for the whole project and stick to that value for all available resources.

# Video container compatibility

Working with video files can be a challenging task if you don't have all the required software to read the data. The problem is that a video file, also known as a container, is a type of file that has two parts:

- Video
- Audio

Each of those data types could come in a compressed or uncompressed format. Usually, a camera or video exporting software will apply some compression to the data to reduce their size.

How big is an uncompressed video file? The exact size will depend on several factors, but you can estimate:

- **FullHD Video (1920 x 1080) at 24 FPS**: 445 GB for 1 hour of video or 127 MB/Second
- **FullHD Video (1920 x 1080) at 60 FPS**: 742 GB for 1 hour of video or 211 MB/Second
- **4K Video (3840 x 2160) at 24 FPS**: 1.33 TB for 1 hour of video or 380 MB/Second
- **4K Video (3840 x 2160) at 60 FPS**: 3.33 TB for 1 hour of video or 950 MB/Second

With such large sizes, it is easy to understand why most video captured with smartphones or consumer cameras has compression. The compression software used for video and audio is what we call the CODEC. It is the same principle as when you get a ZIP file in your email and have to extract the file to get the contents.

If you have a video container, you need the CODEC to both read and compress video and audio files.

What is the best CODEC? There are several options in the market, but for digital video for YouTube or the web, it would be wise to follow some standards. For instance, using H.264 for video and AAC for audio are the recommendations from YouTube in an MP4 (MPEG-4) container.

The good news is that Blender supports MP4 video containers using H.264 and ACC for reading and exporting!

# Data compression types

Another important aspect about a CODEC is the type of compression it applies to data. There are two types of compression available:

- **Lossy compression**: Here we have a process that tries to exclude unnecessary data to save on file size. As a result, files are usually smaller.
- **Lossless compression**: Some compression types will try to shrink data with no data loss, resulting in larger files but with all data intact.

Which one is the compression from an H.264 file? It uses lossy compression, the same that you will also find in a JPEG image file.

That means you must avoid processing the video data as much as possible because, every time you treat the data, your CODEC will try to exclude something to shrink down your file.

# Adjusting the Sequencer zoom and time code

Now that you know more about video containers and compression, we can focus on adding that data to the **Video Sequencer** of Blender. Once you go to the **Add** menu and choose the **Movie** option, pick any MP4 that you want and import it to the **Sequencer**.

After you import the data, you will start to see a video strip, which is the name Blender uses to identify video data in the **Sequencer** (*Figure 1.10*):

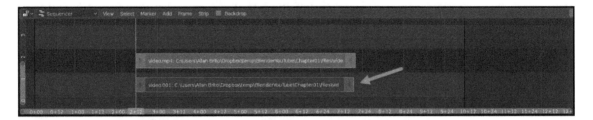

Figure 1.10: Video strip

You probably will start with a limited view of your video file like the one from *Figure 1.10*. Several tools will help you manipulate the zoom or viewing of channels.

The most convenient is the *Home* key on your keyboard. If you press this key, Blender will fit all video strips in your **Sequencer** window.

For more zoom controls, you can hold the *Ctrl* + middle mouse button and move your cursor. If you move up and down, you will adjust the zoom vertically, and going from left to right will adapt it horizontally.

In longer videos, you will probably want to get a broader view of your channels, like the one shown in *Figure 1.11*:

Figure 1.11: Channels with a broader view

Another aspect of the **Video Sequencer** that you will probably want to change is the time code. In case Blender doesn't display seconds as time code, you can enforce that in the **View** menu. There you will find an option called **Show Seconds** that will use the unit instead of frames (*Figure 1.12*):

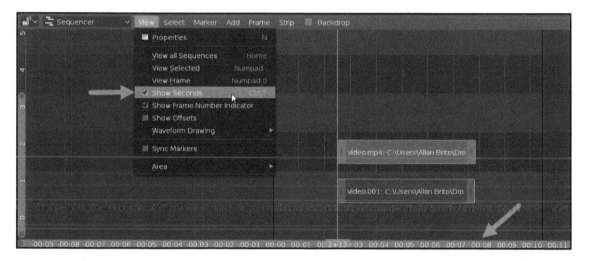

Figure 1.12: Timecode as seconds

The same principle also applies to the **Timeline** window, and you can use the **View** menu and choose **Show Seconds**.

 Use the **Video Editing** workspace to view all options related to video editing from this point forward.

For the times where you have a close view of a strip, a strange time code will appear in your **Sequencer**. It will have a number, a plus sign, and another number. It might look like **0+00**. What does it mean?

Since Blender won't display fractions of a second, it will show the corresponding video seconds plus the frames. A code showing **1+06** means that you are at one second plus six frames.

# Selection of video strips

With a video strip in your **Sequencer**, we can start to manipulate that data to place it in different locations in a project. The first thing we have to learn about video strips is how to select them. In Blender, you must use the right mouse button to select entities.

Once you right-click on any video strip, Blender will immediately display additional information about the video. For instance, you will see the length of a strip and the source name (*Figure 1.13*):

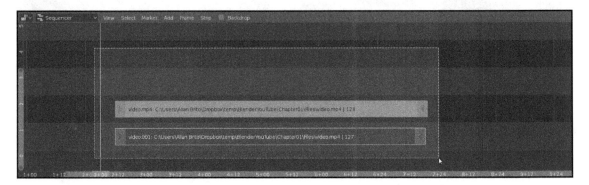

Figure 1.13: Strip selection

After selecting a strip, you can duplicate the content using the *Shift + D* keys. Just press the keys, and you will be able to create a copy of a selected strip. When you press the keys, it will be possible to slide the copy somewhere else in your **Sequencer**. Just move the cursor and left- click at the location you want to place your copied strip.

For the times where you have multiple strips in your **Sequencer**, a few shortcuts will help you manage selection:

- *Shift* + right-click: Add or remove strips to/from selection (for various picks)
- *A* Key: Select all strips in your **Sequencer**
- *Alt + A*: Remove all strips from the selection
- *Alt + I*: Invert the selection of strips

In case you want to make a more extensive selection, you can also use the *B* key to draw a box around any given number of strips. Using the left mouse button, click and drag to draw a box (*Figure 1.14*):

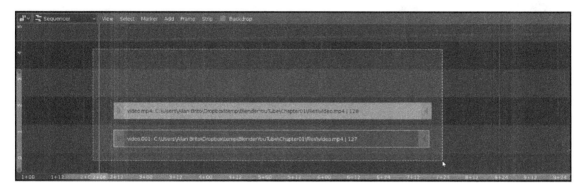

Figure 1.14: Strips selection

One of the benefits of using Blender is the consistency about shortcuts, because you will also be able to use all those options for all other parts of the software. For instance, using *Shift* + right-click will also help you with a selection of objects in 3D modeling or editing animation.

# Transforming video strips

Since your video strips are just 2D objects, we don't need the full range of transformations Blender uses for modeling. Instead, we will only work with the move transformation. To move your strip anywhere in the **Sequencer**, press the *G* key with any given number of selected strips.

After pressing the *G* key, you can move your mouse to relocate the strips, even between channels (*Figure 1.15*):

Figure 1.15: Moving strips

Blender will also display the start and end frames of a strip to help you relocate the video.

In some cases, you can even change some strips, length using the *G* Key. Look at the beginning and end of any strip, and you will see two triangles pointing to the center. They work as location controls. To select them, you can right-click on the triangle, and by pressing the *G* key, you will be able to change only the start or end frames (*Figure 1.16*):

Figure 1.16: Strip length

Use this option with caution on strips with video and audio, because you might either cut or create some blank space. There are other ways to change a strip length. The triangles will work best to set width for static content such as images, text, and effects.

# Saving a video project

How do you save a video project in Blender? To keep your source files and project saved for future reference and updates, you should always save the project. How does Blender handle video files?

Before we discuss how Blender deals with video files, you can save any project by going to the **File** menu and choosing **Save As...** like most other tools.

It will create a file with a `.blend` extension. The file will feature all animation and **Sequencer** data, but none of the external files, unless you explicitly ask Blender to incorporate them into the project.

For instance, suppose you have a project containing two external video files named `video1.mp4` and `video2.mp4`. The first thing you should do is to create a folder in your system to store all the files for that project. Copy all important media to that folder.

In Blender, save the `.blend` file to that folder. Once you import the footage to the **Sequencer**, you will be able to have relative paths to the media. It would be something like `\video1.mp4` and not a full system address.

Why is that important? Because, with relative paths to media files, you can open the project anywhere without any broken links. It will be possible to place the project on network drives or flash storage to move it around.

# Embedding media to Blender files

Another option you should consider is to embed the media to Blender files. To achieve that, you must use an option from the **File** menu in the **External Data** group. There you will find an option called **Pack All into .blend** to add all media to the project file (*Figure 1.17*):

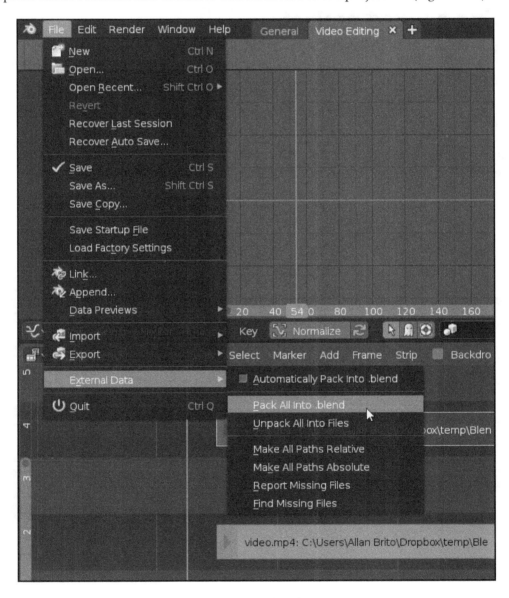

Figure 1.17: External Data options

After using this option, you will have all video footage, audio, and images attached to the blend file. You won't have to worry about any folders or missing links.

The downside of using such an option is the file size. You might end up with a blend file of a few gigabytes in size. To extract the contents of a blend file that has embedded media, use the **Unpack All into Files** option from the same menu.

 If you don't mind about the file size, use the **Automatically Pack into .blend** to make Blender add all external media to the project file. No matter if it is in the same folder, you will have all external media attached to the project.

# Summary

You now have a solid base on how to import and add footage to the **Video Sequence Editor** in Blender. Once you get media as strips, you can use Blender tools to edit and manipulate the content.

The next step is to go even further by editing and rearranging strips any way you want. That is what we will learn in Chapter 2, *Editing and Cutting Video Footage in Blender*.

# 2
# Editing and Cutting Video Footage in Blender

The process of making a video for streaming sites such as YouTube might take several hours to shoot and to get all the content you need. From all those hours of raw footage, you will want to get only the essential parts. In this chapter, you will learn how to use Blender tools to cut, edit, and reorder video footage.

From a simple cut to getting several pieces of footage and stitching them to create a history, you will learn how to do the following:

- Make cuts
- Align parts of a video
- Create a restricted preview
- Use tools to mark your video
- Remove blank spaces from a project

## Technical requirements

You will be required to have Blender 2.80 installed to follow this procedure. Even if you have a later version of Blender, the described example should work with no significant problems.

The media files of this chapter can be found on GitHub:
`https://github.com/PacktPublishing/Blender for-Video-Production-Quick-Start-Guide/tree/master/Chapter02`
Check out the following video to see the procedures in action:
`http://bit.ly/2AAmShI`

# Editing video for YouTube in Blender

A video production project will take a significant amount of time to prepare and also edit because it is common practice in the business to shoot hours of footage and extract only a few minutes.

For instance, you could work on a video interview with an important subject. When you work on that type of production, you will see that people will make pauses or interrupt the discussion in several other ways.

In the end, you will have unedited and raw footage with half an hour of material, which you have to cut and edit until it gets to only 10 minutes.

That is when you will need to use tools to cut, edit, and reorder video footage. In Blender, you will find all those options in the **Video Sequencer**. Since you already know how to use and get footage to the sequencer, we can move forward and edit video footage.

## Using the cut tools for video

A popular tool in any video editing software is the cut option, where you can get any video and split the material into two parts. If you have a video strip in the sequencer, you can also use a similar tool to cut any footage.

Before we proceed, you should have any video footage in your sequencer to use the cut tool successfully.

Once you have a video strip in your sequencer, you will be able to cut the material. Blender has two options for cutting video:

- Hard cut
- Soft cut

The option to activate the cut is in the **Strip** menu shown here (*Figure 2.1*):

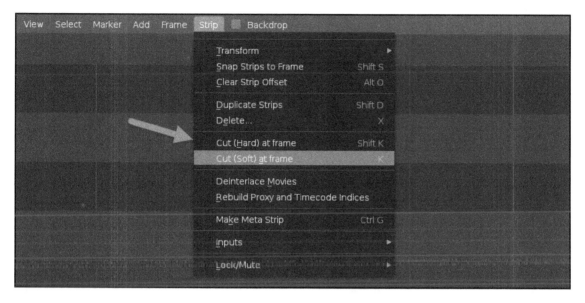

Figure 2.1: Cut options

To cut a video in the sequencer, you must select it first.

 You can also use a shortcut for both cuts with the *K* key (hard cut) and *Shift* + *K* keys (soft cut).

So what is the difference between a hard cut and a soft cut?

Although both options will cut a video strip, you will get a unique resultant **Strip** based on your cut choice. The difference is in the handles at the beginning and end of a strip, which are the two triangles pointing to the center.

If you have an uncut strip that has about 30 seconds of video and use your end handle to extend the length of your footage, Blender will copy the last frame and use it to fill the additional time. The same will happen if you try to extend your strip from the beginning.

That is what will happen to a strip if you use a hard cut (*Shift* + *K* keys).

By going with a soft cut, you will get the option to extend the length of a resultant strip, using the full footage and not a still frame. Look at *Figure 2.2* to see how a soft cut works:

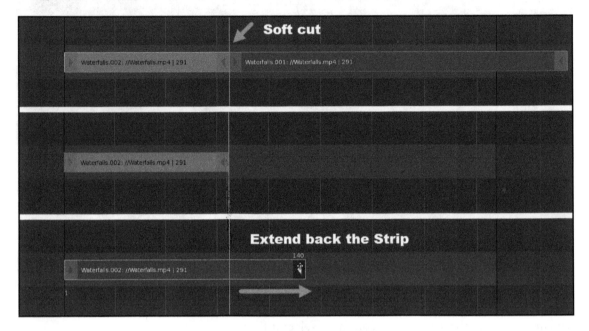

Figure 2.2: Soft cut

It is almost like a mask that Blender applies to the strip, which will hide the undesired parts of your video.

Using a soft cut will enable you to rethink and rework any possible cut you made to a video. If you need more or less from the footage, using the handles and the *G* key will give you the flexibility to change your cut later.

After you cut a strip, you can select the resultant part and either remove it from your sequencer or relocate the content using the *G* key.

Having a strip from a soft cut will enable you to later get additional parts of footage with no need to import it again. Just select an existing strip, and using *Shift* + *D* to duplicate the material, you can use the handles to expand the content.

# Using markers to help edit video

One of the tasks you will want to perform before making a cut in a video is to watch and look for the exact locations where you will split each strip. To find the exact locations, you will have to watch and set key points in your sequencer.

Blender has a tool called marker that might help you locate critical points in a video. The process to add a marker is simple and consists of the following:

1. Triggering the play in your sequencer with either the *Shift* + Space bar keys or the play icon in your **Timeline** window.
2. Press *Shift* + Space bar again to pause in the location you wish to add a marker. You can also click and drag the vertical blue line, to quickly go back and forward in your sequencer.
3. When the blue vertical line is at the exact location, press the *M* key to add a marker (*Figure 2.3*):

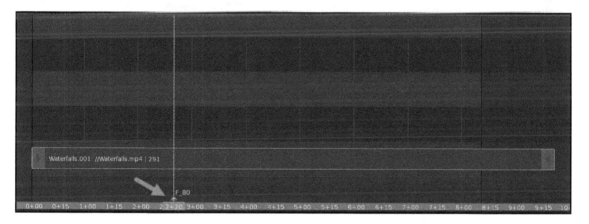

Figure 2.3: Marker in the sequencer

Why should you use markers? The reason to use markers is to make your work easier in editing long video files. If we go back to the example of an interview, you can use the markers to set the exact location where each question starts.

The play button will swap to pause once you trigger the playback. You can also use the button in your timeline to stop.

Furthermore, you can also rename a marker to make it even more useful. You can select a marker by right-clicking on it and pressing *Ctrl + M* to rename your marker (*Figure 2.4*):

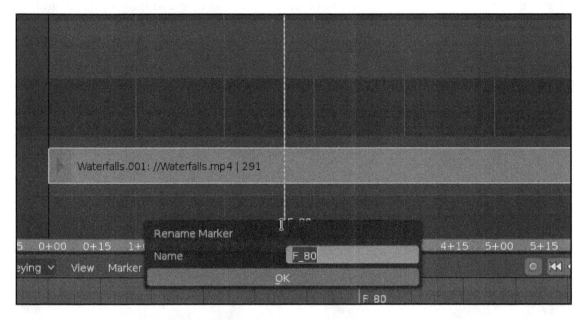

Figure 2.4: Rename marker

With a marker selected, you can even move it to a new location, using the same *G* key that can move a video strip. And if you don't want a marker anymore, press the *X* or *Delete* key to erase it from the sequencer.

The **Video Editing** workspace is perfect for editing a video using the cut tools.

Here is an example in *Figure 2.5* of a sequencer with lots of markers that will help you later to get a quick cut of all the unnecessary parts of a video:

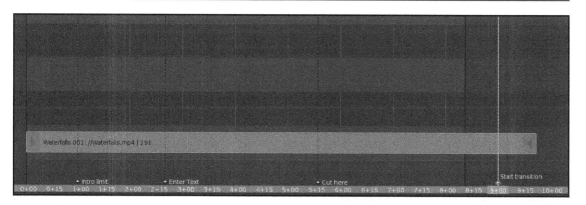

Figure 2.5: Video with markers

The marker menu gives you options such as the following:

- **Duplicate Marker**: If you want to get a marker that has already a name, you can select the marker and use the *Shift* + *D* keys to duplicate.
- **Jump to Previous Marker/Jump to Next Marker**: To quickly navigate between markers, you can use this option in the **Marker** menu.

# Adjusting the project length

When you trigger the playback in your sequencer in Blender to watch the full footage and see possible cut locations, something weird may occur. All of a sudden your playback might stop before it gets to the end of your video.

How do we fix that? Although it may sound like a problem, it is a default behavior from Blender.

Blender will always start a file using a default length for your sequencer, based on the frames set for animation.

Look at the bottom lower-right of your **Timeline** window, and you will see two numeric values for **Start** and **End**, respectively **1** and **250** (*Figure 2.6*):

Figure 2.6: Start and End frames

You will have to change these numbers every time you have a new project. Assuming you are using a frame rate of 30 FPS and you have video footage of 30 seconds, you will need a total of **900** frames (30 seconds x 30 FPS = 900).

Set the **End** to **900** (*Figure 2.7*), and you will be able to play the animation until the end:

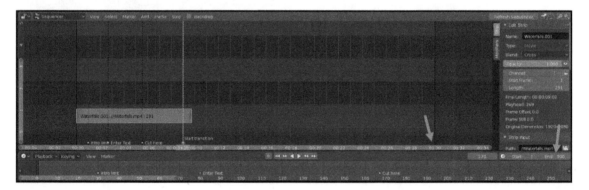

Figure 2.7: End frame

If you don't change this option, Blender will only play back and export the project until the default **End** frame, which is **250**.

Eventually, you will need to change the **End** settings a few times along the editing process of a project. The reason for this is that you might start with a particular number of frames, and after cutting some footage you will shorten the overall length.

For instance, our footage with **900** frames might receive a few cuts and have a reduced length set to **750**. When that happens, you should change the **End** value to match the new range. By doing that, you will ensure a preview of only your final cut and also prepare the project for exporting.

# Using the preview range

In some cases, you may have a long video project that has five minutes or more of content. If you hit *Shift* + Space bar to preview the editing process, you would end up watching the full length.

What if you want to preview a small range of the video? Blender has an option called preview range that could help.

The tool works by limiting the **Start** and **End** frames in your preview only and doesn't change the **Start** and **End** frames from the whole project.

To create a preview range, you can use the *P* key in the sequencer, and draw a square that marks the area where you want to limit your preview. Once you limit the preview, you will see two vertical lines showing the range (*Figure 2.8*):

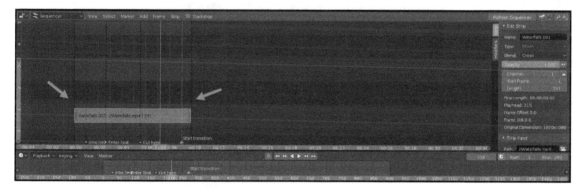

Figure 2.8: Preview range

If you trigger the playback of your sequencer, Blender will only show what's inside the range. Using the *All + P* keys will clear the preview range.

> You can also use the **Frame** menu in the **Sequencer** window to activate the preview range.

# Importing still images

Another essential piece of media that you will want to use in a project is still images. You may want to show a picture or graph to describe a subject or get a single frame from a video. No matter the cause, you can use that type of media in Blender.

To import a still image, you can use the same *Shift + A* keys or **Add** menu in the sequencer, and choose the **Image** option. There you will see the Blender file picker. Choose a single file to use it as a video strip.

In the sequencer, you will see both handlers for the **Start** and **End** of your image strip. The controls and options to manipulate that image are the same from a video (*Figure 2.9*):

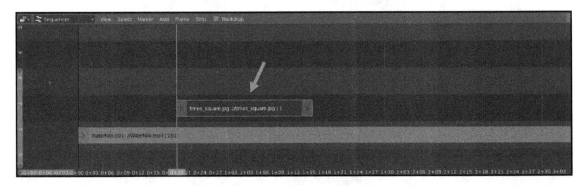

Figure 2.9: Image strip

Besides getting a single image as a strip, you can also use sequences of images and turn them to video. That will come in handy when you have a series of images you shot with a smartphone and want to convert them to video.

To import a sequence of images, you will follow the same steps, with a small difference. When you have the file picker window in Blender, you must select multiple photos. If you have the filenames as a sequence, Blender will set them in order.

How do you select multiple files? You can hold the *Shift* key and right-click on each file or use the *B* key to draw a box around all the files you need. For the cases where you want all the files, press the *Alt + A* keys.

Whenever you have a file selected, you can also unselect it by holding the *Shift* key and right-clicking on the selected item.

> For projects where you have to create video from the 3D content, it is a common practice to render it as an image sequence. There are numerous benefits of using image sequences, such as the possibility to rework and change timing and have a source with a lossless compression as PNG files.

# Using the Snap for video

At some point during a project, you will find yourself with dozens of strips in the sequencer that need some work. A task that might consume a lot of time is the alignment of strips. After a few cuts of a long strip, you will have a lot of blank space in your sequencer, like the one shown in *Figure 2.10*:

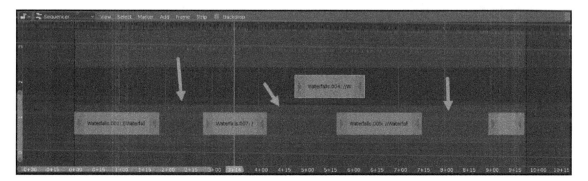

Figure 2.10: Blank space between strips

Using a tool called Snap, you can easily align those strips with the playback head in Blender. The Snap will get a selected strip and align the start frame with the location of your playback head.

How does that work? Simple, you will place the vertical blue line anywhere in your sequencer and select any strip. Press the *Shift + S* keys and the strip will jump to the location. The starting frame of your selected strip will align with the playback head (*Figure 2.11*):

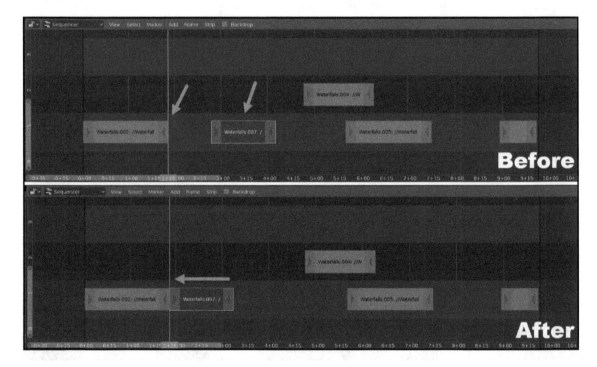

Figure 2.11: Snap tool

If you want to use existing strips for the alignment, a shortcut might become invaluable. By using the *Page Up* and *Page Down* keys, you will jump the playback head to the previous and next strips respectively.

Once you get the playback head at the exact location, select the strip you want to align and press *Shift + S*.

 The Snap tool is also an excellent resource for 3D modeling in Blender, but instead of working with 2D video strips, you will use tridimensional data for alignment.

# Working with gaps for strips

Having the Snap tool is excellent for aligning strips, but it might take you some time to repeat the process for a complex project. Another great way to remove space between strips is with the **Remove Gaps** option.

The tool will work with the *Backspace* key. You must keep the playback head to the left of your strips because Blender will consider all gaps to the right of your vertical line. With the playback head in place, select a strip and press the *Backspace* key.

By doing that, it will trigger the Remove Gaps tool and Blender will move the start of your selected strip to the end of the previous strip (*Figure 2.12*):

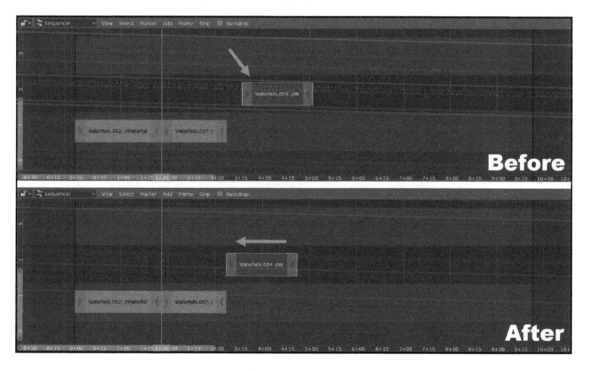

Figure 2.12: Remove gaps option

You can also use the option in the **Strip** menu. In the menu, go to **Transform** and choose **Remove Gaps**.

# Summary

Making all the necessary cuts and adjustments for a video is just the first step of a long process. You now have all the necessary tools to create a simple cut for your projects, even using the famous jump cut from several YouTube videos.

But, for really engaging material on YouTube, you also need animation and a set of effects. In Chapter 3, *Using Properties to Enhance Video*, we will explore the strip properties to change the way each part of your video appears.

# Using Properties to Enhance Video

# 3

Having tools to cut and edit video in Blender is not enough to create high-quality content, and that is where properties will start to make a huge difference. These properties will let you control aspects of videos such as orientation, speed, and colors, which are critical for any production.

In this chapter, you will learn how to use some of the most critical options from the properties of your **Sequencer**, such as the following the following:

- Updating the source file of a strip
- Reversing a video
- Changing orientation
- Adding modifiers
- Using and creating masks

## Technical requirements

You will be required to have Blender 2.80 installed to follow this procedure. Even if you have a later version of Blender, the described example should work with no significant problems.

Check out the following video to see the procedures in action:
http://bit.ly/2PaIYwK

# Properties for video strips in Blender

In the Blender user interface, you will find that most windows will have something called a properties panel. These tabs will give you access to unique properties from objects that will reflect the selected object. For instance, if you have a 3D object selected, you will see properties such as coordinates, scale, and more.

In the **Sequencer**, you will see properties related to video and audio such as Length, Color, and Orientation.

First and foremost, how do you open the **Properties** tab? You will use the same shortcut to open the **Properties** tab in all windows in Blender. Just place the cursor in the window you wish to use and press the *N* key. That will open the properties in a sidebar as shown (*Figure 3.1*):

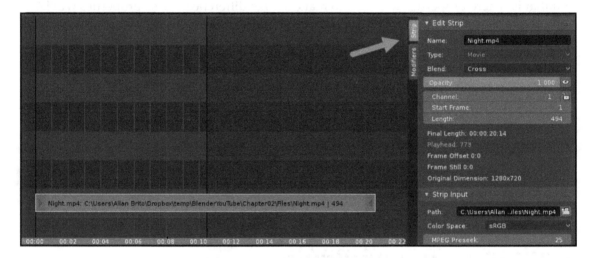

Figure 3.1: Sequencer sidebar

As you will see in *Figure 3.1*, the **Properties** tab will appear on the right-hand side of your window.

You can quickly identify if a window has a **Properties** tab by looking at the upper-right corner. The presence of a small + icon in the upper-right corner of a window shows that you have a **Properties** tab.

The **Sequencer** properties will feature two main options:

- **Strip**: General options for both video and audio
- **Modifiers**: Special modifiers that you can add to any strip to control colors and create effects

To close the **Properties** tab, you can also press the *N* key.

One crucial aspect of the **Properties** tab is that each strip in your **Sequencer** will have unique properties. The values you see in the tab will reflect the selected strip at the moment.

 Blender uses the same **Properties** tab for other windows, and you can access them using the *N* key. Although present in multiple windows, each editor will display unique information related to a selected object.

# Using strip properties

The first set of options you will find in the sidebar are specific to the **Strip**, which will include several alternatives to improve or change your material. In that field, you will see three main groups with options:

- **Edit Strip**: Change the characteristics of your video source such as **Name**, **Channel**, **Blend**, and **Type**.
- **Strip Input**: Manage how your **Strip** uses the external video file reference. Here, you can update or replace the source file and even crop the video.
- **Filter**: Here you will find several options related to the visuals of your video. For instance, you can flip the image and change the color saturation.

Some properties in the sidebar will also offer a way to lock or protect your material if you think that no further editing is necessary. A small padlock icon will appear next to any value that you can secure.

For instance, if you look at the **Channel** option, it has the padlock icon, as shown (*Figure 3.2*):

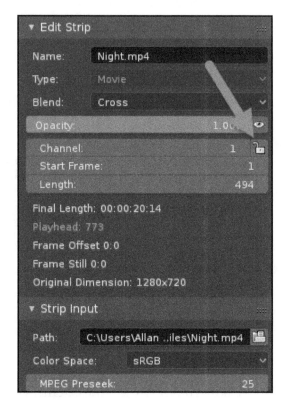

Figure 3.2: Padlock icon

The **Channel** option will let you change the numeric value of a strip. For instance, you can set the channel as **5** and your strip will move to that layer. It is an alternative to the click and drag move, with a precise value.

You can also lock any strip using the *Shift + L* keys. Just select the strips you want to protect and press the keys. To unlock them, use the *Shift + Alt + L* keys.

By turning the lock on, you will block any channel changes. You will still be able to change properties, but you won't be able to slide or move your strip. All locked strips have a series of diagonal lines, making it clear that it has a lock on channel changes.

# Visibility and opacity for video

One of the first properties that you will want to manipulate in the **Sequencer** is the **Opacity**. The **Opacity** of all strips will start with a value of 1.000 meaning you have a video in 100% opacity.

If you set the value to anything below 1, this will make the video transparent (*Figure 3.3*), until it reaches total transparency with a value of 0:

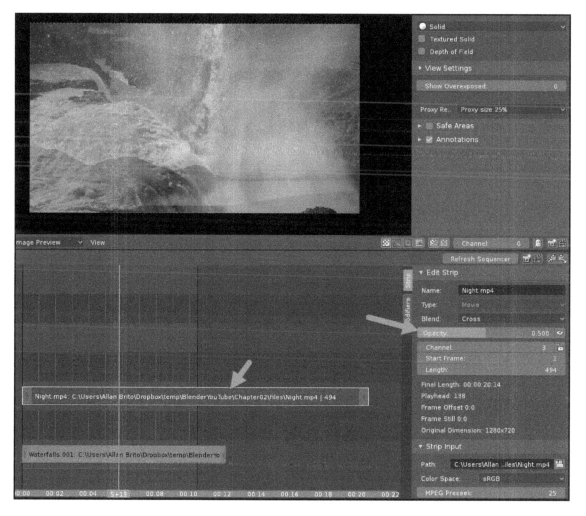

Figure 3.3: Transparent video

Making a video transparent is an alternative to blending multiple footage and might help you in a project. Once you lower the opacity value, any image or video in a lower channel will become visible. If you don't have any content below, your background (black) will appear.

Right next to the **Opacity** controls, you will also see an eye icon. That icon controls the complete visibility of your strip. By clicking on it, you will hide the strip contents.

 Most of the properties can receive keyframes for animation purposes. You can make a strip slowly become invisible as a transition effect, or eventually hide a portion of your video or image.

# Updating the footage source

Although you might not think that changing the footage source of a strip might become useful, you will find that such an option might give you an advantage when you must replace the file with an updated version. For instance, you might have an image that you edited, and it is already aligned, edited, and with effects in your **Sequencer**.

What if you realize that you must remove part of that image? If you could not change the source file, you would have to erase the strips and redo all the editing.

In the **Strip Input** field, you can use the **Path** option to pick a different source file for any **Strip** in the **Sequencer** (*Figure 3.4*):

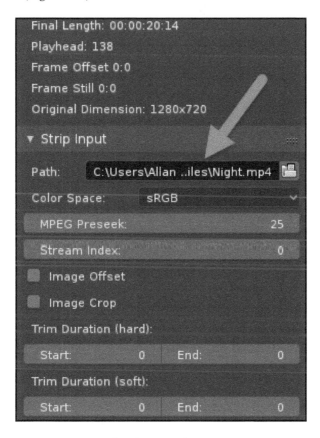

Figure 3.4: Source file for strips

# Cropping and offsetting images and video

Still in the options related to the **Strip Input**, you will find the **Image Crop**, which will help you crop either a video or an image. Once you turn that on, you will see expanded controls with **Top**, **Left**, **Right**, and **Bottom** (*Figure 3.5*):

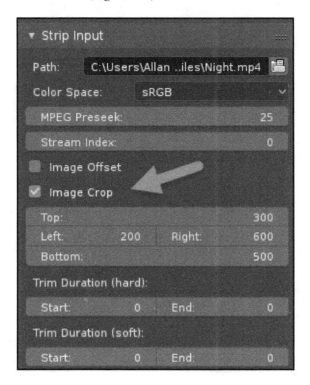

Figure 3.5: Crop image options

You can set the distance in pixels from each border of your video or image for cropping. Blender will apply something like a mask to your strip, and you can always go back to the sidebar and reset the crop area to 0.

 When you crop an image, Blender will stretch the contents to fill the area you are removing.

Another option is the offset to move your images or video on the screen. Why would you want to offset a video?

The option will give you additional controls when you have something like an image with a transparent background, for instance, if you are working in a 1920 x 1080 pixel video and have a picture with that exact size containing your channel logo.

After importing the image, you see the logo at the center of your video screen. Using the offset options, you can slide the image contents. If you enable image offset, two controls will appear:

- **X**: Negative values for left and positive for right
- **Y**: Positive values for up and negative for down

For an image with a logo, you can use those two values to place it in the lower-right corner of your screen.

# Reversing a video

A quick effect that a lot of video producers eventually apply to a project is to invert the playback of footage. In Blender, you can use such an effect by just enabling the **Reverse** in the **Filters** field (*Figure 3.6*):

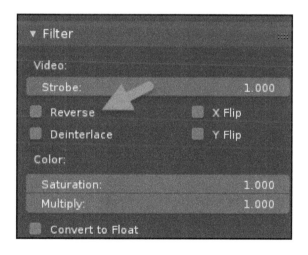

Figure 3.6: Reverse a video

The speed and all other properties will remain the same; only the playback will be backward.

# Flipping videos and images

You may have footage that has an inverted alignment of the camera, which is quite common if you receive footage from an action camera. For instance, you may receive footage from an action camera using a windshield mount in a car. To better align the footage, the operator sets it upside down.

That footage will also be upside down. You will have to flip it to use in your project.

Blender has an option that will enable you to flip video in the **X** (Horizontal) or **Y** (Vertical), as *Figure 3.7* shows:

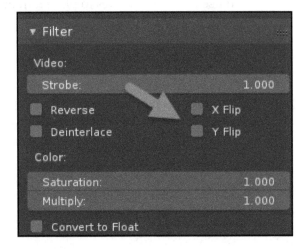

Figure 3.7: Flipping options

The flipping process is simple and doesn't require any additional settings: pick the axis and Blender will invert the video or image.

# Color management and correction

The management of colors in video production is critical for any editor that must blend multiple footage into the same project. You will find that videos from different sources will present differences in color grading and tones.

In the **Sequencer**, in the **Filter** options and **Modifiers**, you will find a wide range of tools that will enable you to manipulate and adjust colors for footage.

Looking at the **Filter** (*Figure 3.7*), you will see the two primary color-related controls:

- **Saturation**: Using this value will change the color saturation of any footage you have selected. What is saturation? It will make the colors with low values dull or make them more vivid with high values. For instance, using a value of 0 will remove all colors, turning the material to grayscale.
- **Multiply**: Here, you will control the overall intensity of color with a multiplier. As a result, you will see the actual colors of footage times related to the value in the **Multiply**. Using high values will make the colors shift to white and make them transparent close to 0.

These are basic controls for colors that you will use for quick corrections.

# Color correction modifiers

In the **Filters** option, you will get basic options for color correction, but to have a wide range of controls for colors, you must use modifiers. If you click on the **Modifiers** tab and the **Add Strip Modifier** button, you will see a list of all available modifiers (*Figure 3.8*):

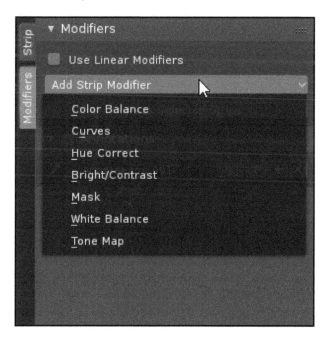

Figure 3.8: Available modifiers for strips

Before we move on to the descriptions of how each modifier works, it is essential to understand how modifiers relate to strips:

- You must select a unique strip to add a modifier
- You can add multiple modifiers to a single strip
- You can stack modifiers on the same strip to create complex color corrections

Once you apply a modifier to a strip, you will have controls, as shown in the following screenshot:

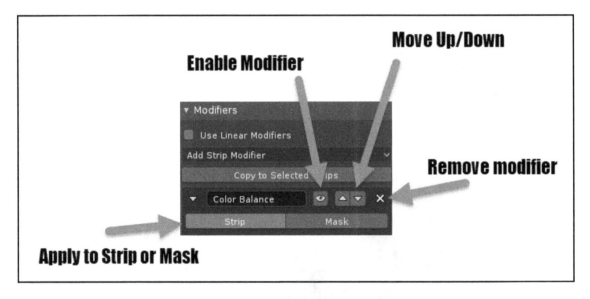

Figure 3.9: Modifiers controls

What can we do with each modifier? Here is a list of the modifiers that can change color data:

- **Color balance**: You will be able to pick a new balance based on lift, gamma, and gain. A color wheel will appear for each field.
- **Curves**: Here we have a tool that strikes fear in most artists, but it is easy to understand. You will get a graph with a diagonal line, starting in the lower-left corner and going up to the upper-right. The lower-left represents dark tones in your image and the upper-right your highlights. At the center, you will get mid-tones. You can shift the colors of your strip by clicking in the curve and dragging a control point toward each zone. For instance, to get more shadows, you can deform the curve toward the lower-left corner.

- **Hue Correct**: In this setting, you will find a graph with a curve containing several control points. There you can click and drag each point toward a tone. The three selectors at the top with the letters H, S, and V let you set the type of correction. With the H you get Hue, and S for saturation, and the V for brightness.
- **Bright/Contrast**: A simple modifier that will give you numeric control over brightness and contrast.
- **White Balance**: If you need to make changes to the white value in your media, use this modifier to set the exact tone for your white.
- **Tone Map**: You can use this modifier to mimic colors from footage with high dynamic range to media that doesn't have that feature.

When should you use each one of these modifiers? That will depend on each project and the color correction required. You may want to create a unique look for a project with warm or cold colors, or just level all tones in your footage from different sources.

## Using masks for effect

By default, Blender will apply modifiers to the strip as a whole unless you limit the effect using a mask. From *Figure 3.8*, you can even see that we have a **Mask** modifier and in *Figure 3.9*, two options at the top for **Strip** and **Mask**.

What is a mask? That is a shape or image that will limit our visibility of a strip. For instance, if you have footage and apply a mask containing a circle at the center, you will only see the part of the video inside the circle area (*Figure 3.10*):

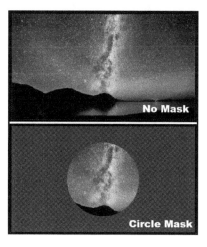

Figure 3.10: Mask example for video

Using a mask in Blender will let you apply color corrections to only part of your strips.

## So how do we create a mask?

To create a mask in Blender, you will have to use a window called **UV/Image Editor**:

1. From anywhere in Blender, you can change the window type to **UV/ Image Editor**. If you are using the **Video Editing** workspace, use the space in the upper-left corner of your interface.
2. Once you have the **UV/Image Editor** window, you must change the mode to **Mask** and add a new mask object using the **New** button (*Figure 3.11*):

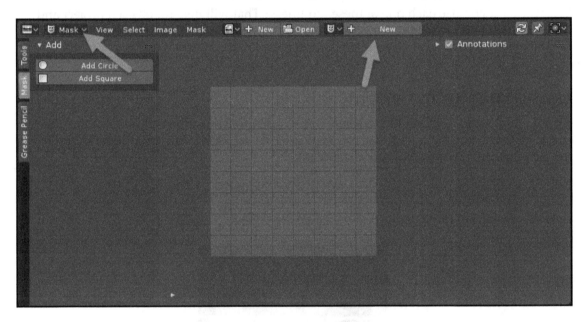

Figure 3.11: Preparing a mask

3. Set a unique name for your mask, and open your toolbar with the *T* key; you can also use the small **+** icon in the upper-left corner of this window. Open the **Mask** tab, and you will get the mask controls (*Figure 3.12*):

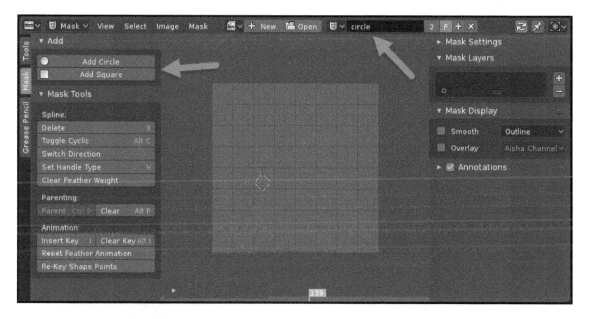

Figure 3.12: Mask controls

4. You will start a mask with either a circle or a square. Use the **Add Circle** button to create a circle mask. To edit and manipulate the mask, you can use the same shortcuts from the **Sequencer**. You can also use the Add menu. With the *G* key, you can move the circle to the center of your mask.

5. Use the *S* key to scale the shape and the *R* key to rotate. Using the numeric controls at the bottom, you can get a perfect alignment to the center using 0.000 for both **X** and **Y**. You can also deform the curve using the control points. Right-click on a point and, using the *G* key, you can change the shape of your circle (*Figure 3.13*):

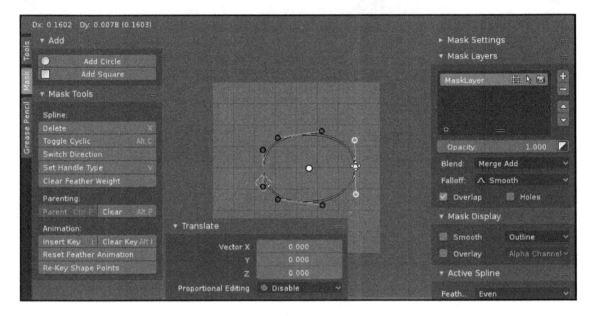

Figure 3.13: Changing the mask shape

You can also change the handle type for each node using the *V* key or the **Set Handle Type** button to:

- **Vector**: You can right-click in each control handler and move them independently. You can get sharp angles from curves. Your node will assume; if you move a handler, it will immediately turn to a **Free** type.
- **Aligned single**: With this option, you will get only a single control node instead of two.
- **Aligned**: Using the aligned handler, you will get handlers that are aligned with each other, generating smooth curves.
- **Free**: Just like the **Vector**, we have independent handlers that can create sharp angles. The main difference from the **Vector** is that a **Free** handler will maintain the original aspect of a handler.

After setting the mask just the way you need, it is time to use the shape to limit either an effect or a modifier. Before we get to the modifiers, note that you will have to select the mask by its name. At the top of your **UV/ Image Editor**, you will see the mask name (*Figure 3.14*):

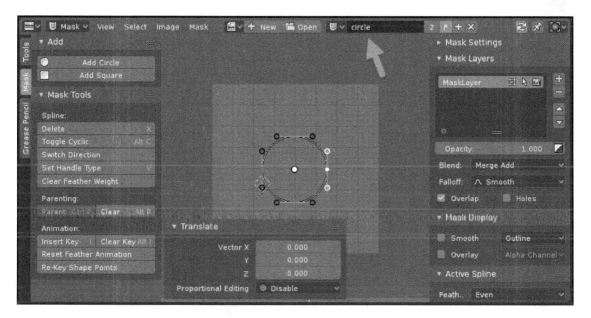

Figure 3.14: Mask object name

You can click on that name and change it to anything you like.

In the modifiers, we can use the mask to limit the area of effect by choosing it as the data type for any modifier (*Figure 3.15*):

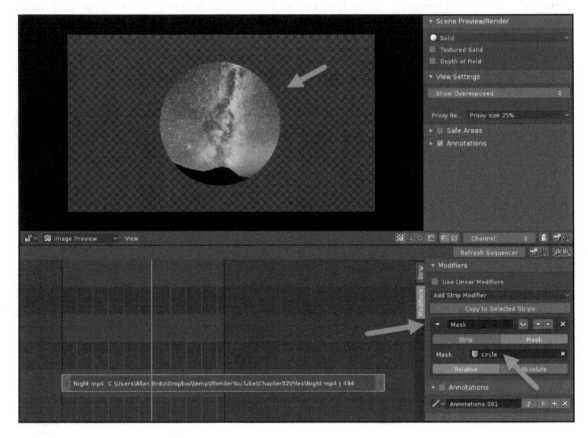

Figure 3.15: Using masks for modifiers

You can get multiple masks in the same Blender project, which is a great reason to set unique names for each mask you create.

You can use a mask to hide parts of a video or image. Just use mask modifiers to display only the contents inside the mask area.

## Copying modifiers to strips

Having modifiers for making the color correction is an excellent resource for any video-related project in Blender, but you might give yourself a problem. Each modifier will work on a single strip. What if you have a project with dozens of strips?

In that case, you can use a button called **Copy to Selected Strips** right below the modifier selector.

Using that option will get all modifiers from the active strip and copy them to all other selected strips. But, what is an active strip?

In Blender, you will find the concept of the active selected object. When you pick multiple objects in Blender, the last one in your selection will be active. For instance, you can use the *B* key to select dozens of strips at once and leave the strip with the desired modifiers out of the selection.

Once you get all strips selected, hold the *Shift* key and right-click on the strip that has all modifiers. It will become the active strip from the selection. Click on **Copy to Selected Strips** and Blender will replicate all modifiers, from the active strip to the selected strips.

That is a great way to make a color correction in one part of your footage, and replicate the settings to all other shots.

# Summary

With properties, you can make a lot of changes and enhancements to video, images, and also sound. Now that you have all the necessary information about properties, we can move further to add animation to our projects.

When you put together animation and properties, you will find an incredible technique for enhancing your videos. In Chapter 4, *Animated Properties for Video Effects*, you will learn how to add keyframes and make animations using properties.

# 4
# Animated Properties for Video Effects

Animation is a great way to enhance any video-related project, and in this chapter, you will learn how to apply animation to video. The animation may come as elements such as images or by changing properties over time.

Here is what you will learn:

- Creating and managing keyframes
- Using effect strips for video
- Changing visual aspects of video
- Adding an overlay animation
- Including an animated watermark to a video

## Technical requirements

You will be required to have Blender 2.80 installed to follow this procedure. Even if you have a later version of Blender, the described example should work with no significant problems.

The media files of this chapter can be found on GitHub:
https://github.com/PacktPublishing/Blender-for-Video-Production-Quick-Start-Guide/tree/master/Chapter04
Check out the following video to see the procedures in action:
http://bit.ly/2Pbi3RD

# Working with animation for properties

The properties for video strips are an excellent resource for video production in Blender, but they will become much more useful with animation. Blender has a full animation system, and you can animate almost all properties.

How do you create animation? Blender is interpolation-based and will work with keyframes to make animation. In interpolation, you will need at least two keyframes in different locations in your timeline. If those keyframes have properties with unique values, Blender will calculate all intermediate frames to make a transition.

For instance, you can start in frame 1 with a strip having an opacity of 0. Add another keyframe for that strip in frame 48 and set the opacity to 1.

That will mean you have a strip starting with full transparency and, in 48 frames, which is about two seconds, it will become fully visible. The transformation won't be instantaneous, but gradual. Blender will do the math and create all opacity changes between frames 2 and 47.

# Making transparency animations

Since we just mentioned an opacity animation, we can start describing properties animation using that same example. You can start with any strip that you like, no matter if that is a video or image.

Hereafter, I will assume you will use the **Video Editing** workspace. If you don't remember how to use workspaces, go back to Chapter 1, *Blender as a Video Editor for YouTube*, and take a look at the workspace description.

How do you create an animation?

1. Once you have a strip in your **Sequencer**, using either your playback head or the **Timeline** window, set the actual frame to **1**. Click and drag with the mouse or use your **Current Frame indicator**, by typing the exact number, as shown here (*Figure 4.1*):

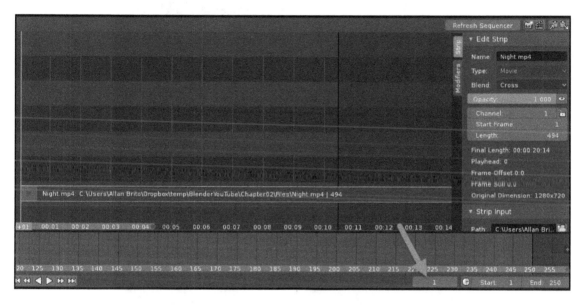

Figure 4.1: Current frame indicator

2. With the current frame set as 1, you can select the strip and open your sidebar using the *N* key. There you will locate the **Opacity** control, and change it to 0.

3. The critical step now is to add a keyframe. In Blender, you can add a keyframe to properties using either the *I* key or with a right-click. To use them, you should place the mouse cursor over the property, and press the key. If you right-click on the property, Blender will display more options, among them the **Insert Keyframe** to create a new keyframe at the location (*Figure 4.2*):

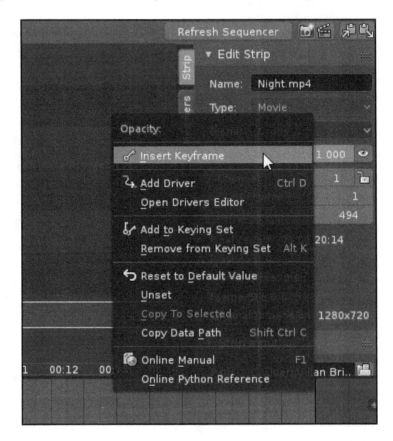

Figure 4.2: Keyframe options

4. You now have a keyframe at position 1! Next, set the current frame to 48 and change your opacity to 1 in the same strip. Insert another keyframe for the opacity. If you go back to frame 1 and press play, you will see the strip starting with full transparency and slowly appearing in two seconds!

One thing you should remember from the process is the order to insert keyframes:

1.  Set the position of your current frame
2.  Change the property value you want to animate
3.  Insert the keyframe

If you skip step 1 and go straight to the property value, you will eventually overwrite an existing keyframe. You can always use *Ctrl + Z* to undo such operations in case that happens.

Following the necessary steps, you can add keyframes and animation to almost any property in Blender. But, before we move on to effect strips, we should look at a few things related to animation, especially in the interface.

Look at *Figure 4.3* for a few details:

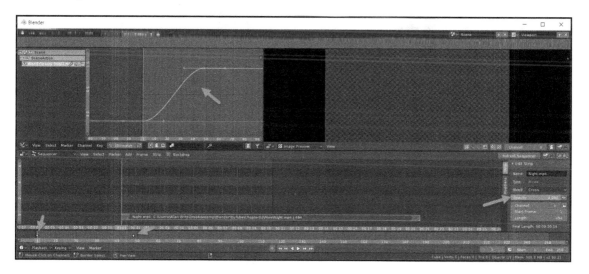

Figure 4.3: Video editing with keyframes

Here are a few points you should look at in the interface after you add keyframes:

*   In the **Timeline** window, you will see keyframes as orange diamonds.
*   The background color of any property with keyframes will change. On the frame with a keyframe it will become yellowish, and between keyframes, it will have a green color.

- The graph editor will display the keyframes as a curve, which you can edit later. Place the mouse in that window and press the *Home* key on your keyboard to view all keyframes. You can also use the **View** menu and choose **View All**.
- Blender will only display that information in the UI for selected strip.

To create animations, you must have two keyframes with different values for properties. However, sometimes you may want to create a sequence of keyframes that share the same values.

In Blender, you will see a thick solid line connecting keyframes that share the same value. For instance, I took the example from the opacity animation and added another keyframe at frame **60**, using the value of **1**. The **Timeline** will display a thick line connecting them (*Figure 4.4*):

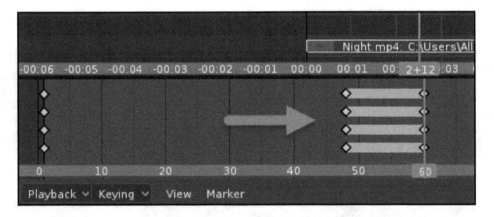

Figure 4.4: A solid line connecting keyframes

By hitting play, you won't see any changes in animation, because both keyframes share the same values.

 Having two keyframes with the same property value is a technique for making a still animation.

# Using effect strips

Animations and keyframes will give us lots of possibilities for creative presentations and effects for video, but you could do a lot more by adding some built-in effects. Blender has a full collection of strip effects that you can associate to an existing media. They are all available in the **Add** menu in **Effect Strip** (*Figure 4.5*):

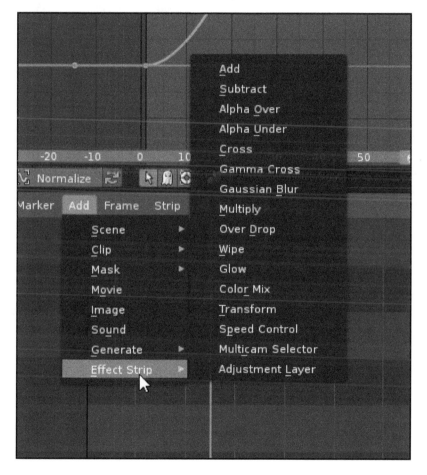

Figure 4.5: Effect strip

These strips work by adding unique visual effects to any particular type of media and, in some cases, multiple strips.

For instance, you can select an existing strip, and from the **Add** menu choose the **Gaussian Blur** in your **Effect Strip** selector. After adding an **Effect Strip**, it will become part of your selected media and will share and follow the same size. You will see another strip representing the effect, as shown (*Figure 4.6*):

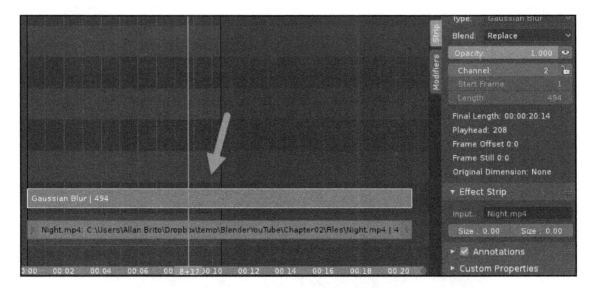

Figure 4.6: Gaussian Blur

If you either resize or move your strip, the effect will follow and keep the same length as the media. To change the settings for most effect strips, you will use the sidebar. Right-click on the **Effect Strip** and you will see the settings in the **Effect Strip** field (*Figure 4.7*):

Figure 4.7: Effect Strip options

Using values of **40** units for **Size X** and **Size Y** will add a significant amount of blur to any media. A value of 0 means no blur at all, and, like all properties, you can add keyframes in your **Size X** and **Size Y** to start a video with a blurred image, and make it crisp with time.

# Types of effect strip

Besides the **Gaussian Blur** effect, you'll find a long list of options for effect strips in Blender. The procedure to add and edit each one of them is similar to what we already did with the **Gaussian Blur**. However, some of the effects will require you to select two strips instead of one.

The reason for this is the fact that some effects will depend on multiple selections. For instance, with the Cross effect, you can create a visual transition called **crossfade** (*Figure 4.8*):

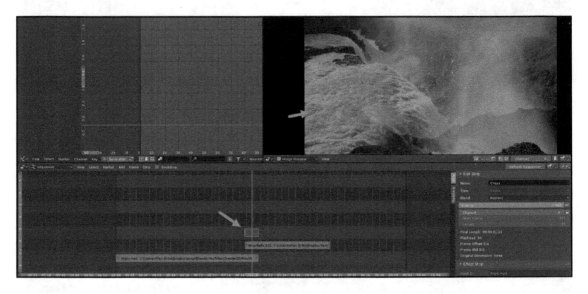

Figure 4.8: Crossfade effect

If you try to apply an **Effect Strip** that requires two or more strips, Blender will display an error, asking you to use the correct number of strips.

In the following list, you will see a description for each of the effects available:

- **Add**: Using this effect will enable you to add the color of another strip to another. For instance, you can add an image that has an exciting color tone to a video. You must select two strips for it to work.
- **Subtract**: Going in the opposite direction from the **Add** effect, you can remove colors from a strip using another image.

- **Alpha Over/Alpha Under**: Using these two effects will enable you to see through transparent pixels of footage, for instance, if you have a PNG file with a transparent background in channel **2** and a video in channel **1**. Apply the **Alpha Over** effect to the image strip, to effectively make the pixels transparent. That is a great way to add a watermark effect to videos.

- **Cross**: Just like we mentioned before, the **Cross** effect will create a fade-in and fade-out transition, causing the first video to disappear slowly and the next to appear from full transparency. To use the effect, you must select two strips that have overlapping frames.

- **Gamma Cross**: Using the **Gamma Cross** effect will create a better-looking fade effect between media, based on the colors of the two selected strips.

- **Multiply**: Use this effect to multiply values of two colors. You can use this effect to soften high-saturation images using another image as a reference. You will need two strips to use the **Multiply** effect.

- **Over Drop**: The **Over Drop** effect works like a **Cross** transition with transparency. You will need two overlapping strips, of which the top strip must have transparent pixels in the background. Using the effect will create a gradual fade using the transparent pixels.

- **Wipe**: Another option for transitions is the **Wipe** effect which will use the overlapping space between two strips. It works by uncovering the second video using a vertical division line.

- **Glow**: A simple effect that will create a **Glow** effect for your video, making it look brighter. You will have controls such as **Boost Factor** and **Quality** to control the quality of your end effect.

- **Color Mix**: Using this effect on two strips will blend their colors.

- **Transform**: In the same way you would make transformations to 3D or 2D objects in a graphic design application, you can also apply that to strips. After adding the effect to a strip, you will have options to change position, rotation, and scale of a video.

- **Speed Control**: If you are trying to create an effect for video where it suddenly becomes faster or slower, you will need this effect. With the speed control, you can manipulate the playback speed of any strip.

- **Multicam Selector**: For projects related to 3D animation using multiple cameras, you can get easy control over the active view using this effect.

- **Adjustment Layer**: If you need to apply an effect or adjustment to multiple strips at once, you can use an **Adjustment Layer**. It works by controlling all strips below the effect. For instance, if you create an **Adjustment Layer** on channel **8**, everything below that channel will receive the same effects and modifiers applied to the strip effect.

Each of those effects will help you to achieve a specific visual in the Blender Sequencer Editor. Almost all parameters from those effects can also receive keyframes for animation purposes.

Some of the options, such as the **Alpha Over** and **Alpha Under**, will allow you to have great flexibility by blending still images to videos.

# Mixing effects for overlay animations

If you look at the long list of effects available in the Sequencer Editor, you will probably find yourself thinking about how to use them in practice. To show a practical example, we can create a short animation that will blend text and graphics using effects.

As a result, you will get an overlay animation for video, which is quite common in productions for YouTube and other video streaming services. What is an overlay animation? When you get video footage and need to add something such as an animated watermark, you will have an overlay animation.

For the following example, we will use an image that has both graphics and text. The file is in PNG format and has a transparent background (*Figure 4.9*):

Figure 4.9: PNG file for overlay

You can get any video footage to apply the effects of an overlay animation.

 You can download both the image and video footage used in this example from the resources for this chapter.

The first thing to do is to add both the video on channel **3** and our image in channel **1** of the **Sequencer** (*Figure 4.10*):

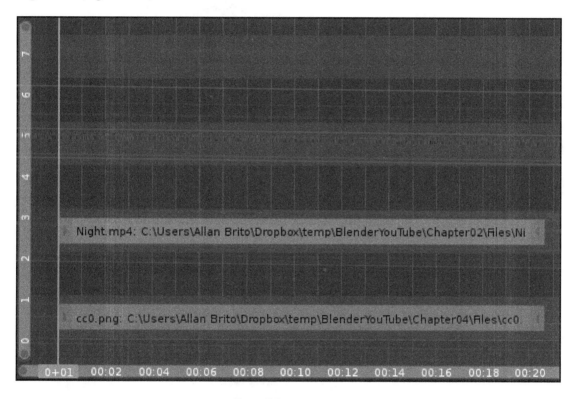

Figure 4.10: Sequencer with strips

Why do we need to place the video on channel **3** and image on channel **1**? Wouldn't it be better to put the picture on top of the video for an overlay?

The reason we have to place an image in a lower channel is that Blender will apply effects to everything below an **Effect Strip**. If you want to move the graphics only, it must go below the video.

Otherwise, using a **Transform** effect would move both image and video.

But, how can we see the graphics?

1. Simple: we can change the **Blend** type of the video in the properties to **Screen**. That will enable us to look through the footage to anything below (*Figure 4.11*):

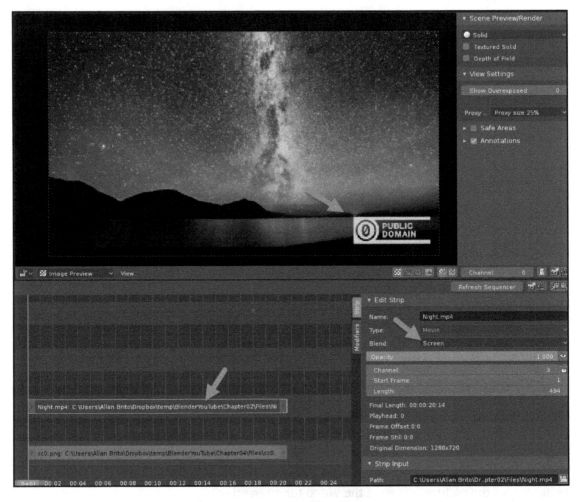

Figure 4.11: Blend type

2. If you look at the preview, you will see that we have the graphics and text in the lower-right corner of the screen. The animation we will create uses the graphics as a watermark, but we don't want a simple fade-in effect.

3. We will start the graphics outside the screen area, to the right, and make an animation where the image will slide in and stop in the lower-right corner.

4. To do that, we will need a **Transform** effect. Apply the effect to the image, which will enable us to move the image.

5. Select the **Transform** effect from your Sequencer and, in the sidebar, locate the **Effect Strip** options. In the **Position** options, you have to change the **X** value.

6. However, since we already have the image in the exact location where our animation will finish, we can start by adding a keyframe at this position at frame **30**. Move your playback head to frame **30** and right-click at the **X** position from your **Effect Strip** options and choose **Insert Keyframe** (*Figure 4.12*):

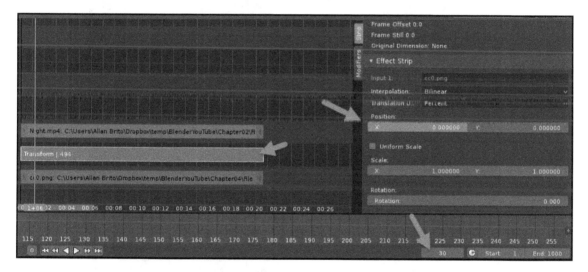

Figure 4.12: Inserting a keyframe

7. Now, we have to make the animation for the starting location of our image. Go back to frame **1** and change the **Effect Strip** options to make your **X** value become **30**. Using that value will slide your image to the right and place it outside of the screen.

8. Add another keyframe by right-clicking on it, and you will have an animation!

Following this exact procedure will generate a strange result. You will see that Blender will fill the transparent pixels from our image with a solid color. The reason for this is that they can only be opaque or transparent. It is like saying something can be either 0 or 1. What if you need something like 0.5?

To enable smooth transitions with effects, you have to turn your image data to **Float**. Just locate the checkbox in the properties and enable **Convert to Float** (*Figure 4.13*):

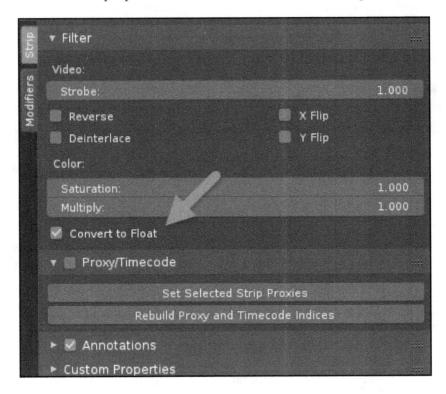

Figure 4.13: Convert to Float

If you press the *Shift* + *s*pace bar keys, you will see the results in your preview window (*Figure 4.14*):

Figure 4.14: Previewing the animation

For the times you have to create an animation like this one, you can always start adding the keyframes for the final position to save some time.

# Summary

The animations we create with effect strips in Blender can surely help to create compelling videos, and you now can add and manage keyframes to most properties in Blender. But, we can do a lot more with animation!

In Chapter 5, *Creating Intro Videos for YouTube with Text and Motion Graphics*, you will see how to create motion graphics with Blender by mixing not only effect strips, but also 3D content! As a result, we will make an intro video for a YouTube channel.

# 5
# Creating Intro Videos for YouTube with Text and Motion Graphics

One of the most significant advantages of using Blender to produce any content related to video is the immediate availability of a full-featured 3D editor. Whenever you need to create animation and blend that with 3D content, all you have to do is change the editor type.

In this chapter, you will learn how to use some of the 3D tools in Blender to emulate a bi-dimensional animation editor with an orthographic camera. From that orthographic camera, we will add text, graphics as textures, and an animated background.

Here is what you will learn:

- Managing cameras in Blender
- Creating and setting up an orthographic camera
- Adding and editing 3D text
- Assigning textures to objects
- Using transparent textures for enhanced graphics
- Creating animations from 3D objects
- Editing animation speed
- Using multiple scenes in the Sequencer

# Technical requirements

You will be required to have Blender 2.80 installed to follow this procedure. Even if you have a later version of Blender, the described example should work with no significant problems.

The media files of this chapter can be found on GitHub:
`https://github.com/PacktPublishing/Blender-for-Video-Production-Quick-Start-Guide/tree/master/Chapter05`
Check out the following video to see the procedures in action:
`http://bit.ly/2FNvTtU`

# Creating an intro for YouTube

An intro clip for a channel or video is significant as it presents valuable information to anyone watching your content. You can present your brand, subject, or any other relevant information for the audience.

In most video editing software, you will find some tools and options to add text and graphics to video, and Blender is no different. However, we must make a few adjustments before some particular types of projects.

You will need a 2D space to create text animations and also set the Blender 3D camera with an orthographic projection. The intro can hold several types of visual content from images to full 3D models. But, in our case, we will use title text and a fictional logo for our channel.

# Making a storyboard for your animation

The first step in the process of getting an intro video for your projects is to arrange a storyboard to guide the production. Using a simple approach for the storyboard will allow you to focus solely on production and worry less about what the final product will look like.

In our case, we will use a simple design for the intro video to show the following parts:

- Title text
- Logo
- Animated background

If you look at a static version of the intro video, you will see something similar to *Figure 5.1*:

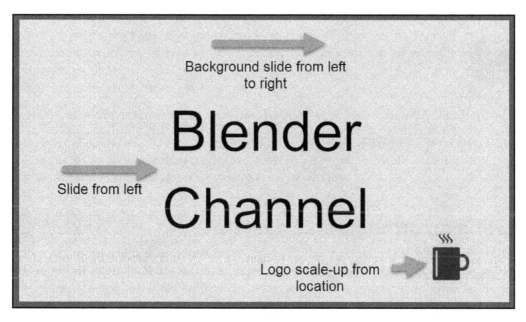

Figure 5.1: Intro video layout

The title text we can create inside Blender itself uses some of the tools available for 3D content creation, and our logo is a texture that we will apply to a 3D plane. We will make it use transparent pixels to only display the necessary shape.

What about the background? We will use another plane with a texture, but with a loop animation to create a much better-looking video.

## Preparing Blender for animation

Until this point, we made all the designs for our projects using only the **Video Sequencer Editor**, and it worked great for our purposes. But if you want to use the full power of Blender, we must also use the **3D Editor** and it's capabilities.

With that in mind, we must prepare Blender to create all the necessary elements to make our intro video.

Start a new project in Blender or press the *Ctrl + N* keys to create a new file and choose **General** from the options.

If you have an actual project in Blender that you don't want to lose, you can always use the **File** menu to save the project before starting a new one.

Once you get to the Blender default screen, we can start preparing the project.

A critical step for the project is the setup of our user interface to have something close to a video editor space. We will set the view to the top with an orthographic projection to simulate a 2D space. That view will become essential to blend our results with a video later.

## Creating an orthographic camera

Regarding rendering 3D content in Blender, we must prepare our space to follow a simple rule. The software will only render 3D content visible to the active camera. In the default scene, you already have a camera to use, and we need to relocate it to the top.

How do you do that? The first step is to set our view to the top using the *7* key from your numeric keyboard, or go to the view menu and choose **Viewpoint | Top**.

For keyboard shortcuts related to 3D navigation to work, you must place the mouse cursor over the **3D View** window. That will set the window as active.

Look to the top-left corner of your **3D View** and you will see the name **Top Perspective**. It means our view is successfully at the top. But we still have to change the camera.

There is a shortcut in Blender that will make any active camera move and adapt to the current viewing angle you have in the **3D View**. Press *Ctrl + Alt + Numpad 0* to move the camera. You will also find an option in the **View** menu to perform the same alignment. Use **View | Align View | Align Active Camera to View**.

After aligning the camera, you will see a rectangular box on your screen. That is your camera (*Figure 5.2*):

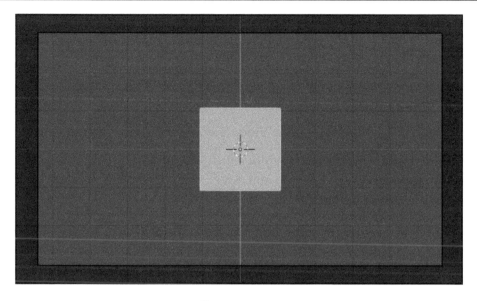

Figure 5.2: Camera view

Now, we must change the camera projection from perspective to orthographic. Select the camera with a right-click in any part of the rectangular shape representing the camera, and look for the camera icon in the **Properties** window. There you will find the options related to the camera.

Using the **Type** option, you can swap between perspective and orthographic (*Figure 5.3*):

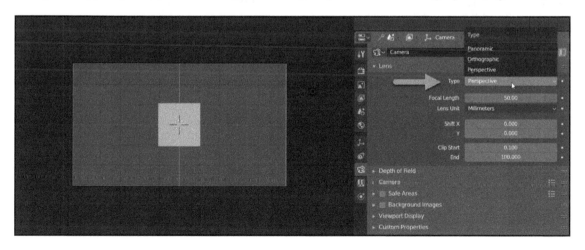

Figure 5.3: Changing camera type

Below the **Type** option, you will also find the **Orthographic Scale**, which you can use to control the size of objects in the orthographic projections. Set that value to 20 and turn on the **Safe Areas** to display a dashed area inside the camera field of view.

The **Safe Areas** will work as a guide to place content for video and animation about possible visible areas on different displays.

You can use the same shortcuts from the Video Sequencer Editor to manipulate the scene:

- *Shift+* **middle mouse button**: Move the view (pan)
- **Mouse scroll wheel**: Zoom in and out
- **Middle mouse button**: 3D orbit the scene

 If you accidentally move out from the camera view, you can always return by pressing the *Numpad 0* to go back to the active camera.

# Working with 3D text in Blender

We now have an environment in Blender that will give you a 2D view of your 3D space, which will allow you to create all kinds of animations to use in video projects. This is something that you will find in tools such as Adobe After Effects or Apple Motion.

Since we won't need the default cube from Blender, you can right-click on that object and erase it with either the *X* key or *Delete*.

Our intro will need some text to show the channel name, and we can use the *Shift + A* keys to call the **Toolbox** floating menu. After pressing the keys, you will see several options, and among them is the **Text** option. Choose **Text**, and you will see a default text object with **Text** as content (*Figure 5.4*):

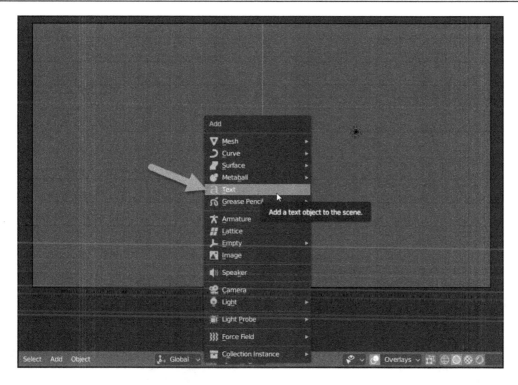

Figure 5.4: Text object

How do you change the text content? Regarding 3D content in Blender, you have to deal with work modes to change particular types of objects; for instance, we are now in **Object Mode**. To change your text, you must go to **Edit Mode**.

Press the *Tab* key with the text selected or use the selector in the lower-right corner of your **3D View** (*Figure 5.5*):

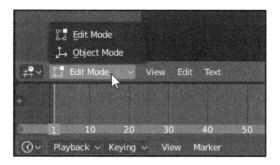

Figure 5.5: Using Edit Mode

Once in **Edit Mode**, you can use the *Backspace* key to erase the text and type anything you need. In our case, we can type `Blender Channel`. After the Blender word, you can

press *Enter* to add a line break.

What about alignment and fonts? You can

use the **Properties** window where you will find an icon pointing to text options. There you can use the **Alignment** options to center the text.

For the font, you will also find a section called **Font**. Use the small folder icon to locate and open a font file for Blender. For instance, I located `arial.ttf` on my computer and Blender is using the font for our text (*Figure 5.6*):

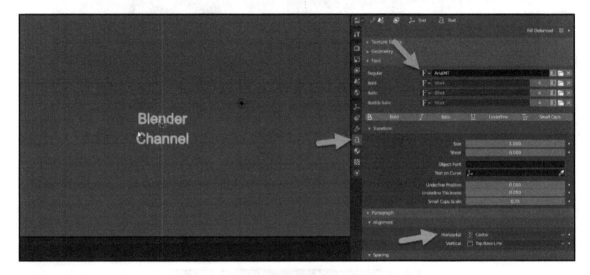

Figure 5.6: Font and alignment

When you have the text ready, go back to **Object Mode** using the same selector or the *Tab* key.

Using the controls on the **Toolbar**, you can **Move**, **Rotate**, and **Scale** the object. Try to center the text and adjust the size of your text to match *Figure 5.7*:

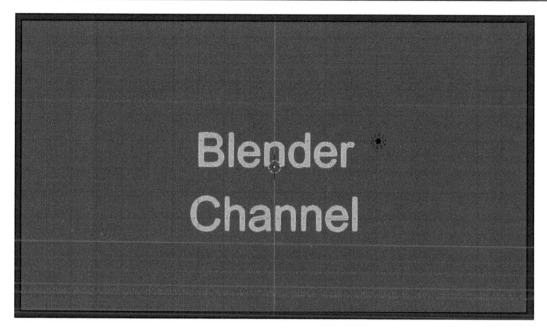

Figure 5.7: Text location

You can also turn on some visual guidelines to help you find the center of your framing. In the **Properties** window, locate the **Viewport Display.** Find the **Composite Guides** and turn on **Center** and **Center Diagonal**. The options appear in the camera settings.

# Adding graphics as textures

To add graphics as textures, we will need to open each image in Blender and create 3D objects that will receive those images as textures. Before you create an object to receive those images in Blender, we need a critical piece of information. You need the image dimensions.

Why? To avoid any potential distortions on images in Blender, we have to match the proportions for each graphic. For instance, we have a logo for the channel with 745 x 750 pixels. If you apply that logo to a square 3D plane, it will have a small distortion.

How do you find image's dimensions? Go to the file manager of your system and right-click on the image file and ask for **Properties**. There you will find properties such as dimensions. Here is an example of the details from a Windows 10 system (*Figure 5.8*):

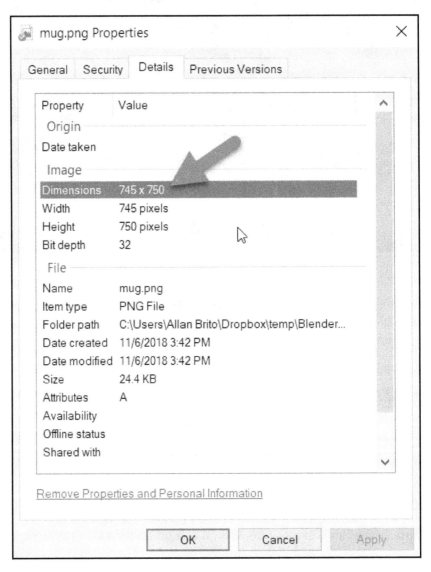

Figure 5.8: Image dimensions

With the dimensions in mind, we can create an object in Blender.

If you are on a Mac, you can use *Cmd* + *I* to open a similar panel when selecting an image file.

In the **3D View**, you can press the *Shift* + *A* keys and choose **Mesh** | **Plane**. It will create a square 3D plane. Now, press the *N* key to open the **Properties** sidebar in your **3D View** and locate the dimensions for the plane.

Change the dimensions to become 7.45 for **X** and 7.50 for **Y**. We only need the proportions to be the same (*Figure 5.9*):

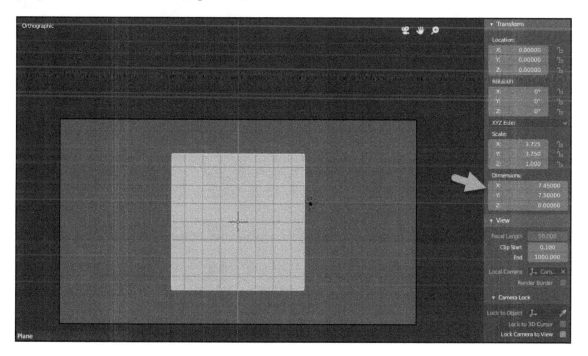

Figure 5.9: Plane proportions

The next step is to create a material for the plane. In the properties, the window adds new material to the plane using the **New** button (*Figure 5.10*). Change the material shader to **Diffuse BSDF**. Click on the **Principled BSDF** name and pick **Diffuse BSDF** instead:

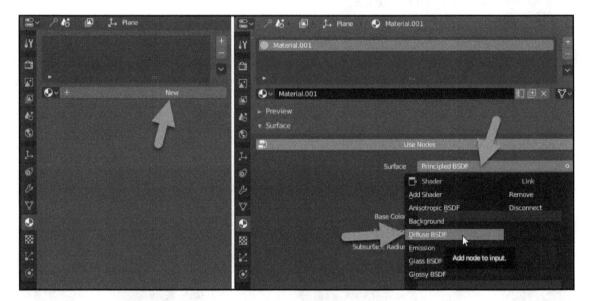

Figure 5.10: Adding new material

For the color, choose black.

We will need a material to assign a texture, and that is our next move. Using the space of your **Timeline** window, change the window type to **Shader Editor**.

There you will see Blender's Visual Material Editor. Using the *Shift + A* key, add the following nodes to the **Shader Editor**:

- **Shader | Transparent BSDF**
- **Shader | Mix Shader**
- **Texture | Image Texture**

You will see unconnected nodes floating in your window. In the **Image | Texture** node, use the **Open** button to get the mug.png file from your hard drive.

Although the **Shader Editor** might look complicated to use, it is incredibly easy once you learn how to connect nodes. To connect two nodes, you can click and drag from an output socket on the right to an input socket on the left. Use the colors of each circle as a reference.

For instance, connect the color output from the **mage Texture** (yellow) to the color input of your **Diffuse BSDF** on the left.

Hold the *Ctrl* key and click and drag with the left mouse button to cut the connection from the **Diffuse BSDF** to the **Material Output**. Then, connect the **Mix Shader** to the **Material Output** (green). Connect the **Diffuse BSDF** to the lower input socket of your **Mix Shader**, and the **Alpha** from your **Image Texture** to the **Fac** of your **Mix Shader**.

Finally, you can connect the **Transparent BSDF** output to the middle input socket of your **Mix Shader**. You will get an arrangement similar to what *Figure 5.11* shows:

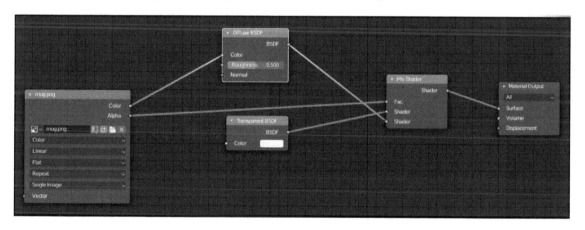

Figure 5.11: Material nodes

What do all these nodes mean? We are using an **Image Texture** and applying it as visible content (**Diffuse BSDF**) of our material. And based on transparent pixels from the object, we are showing a fully transparent material (**Transparent BSDF**), only at places where our image has transparent pixels (**Alpha | Fac**).

Finally, using the *S* key, you can shrink down the plane and move it to the lower-right corner of your screen and apply the scale with *Ctrl + A*.

Whenever you make a scale transformation that later will receive keyframes, it is wise to apply the scale with *Ctrl + A*. That will remove any scale factors from the object and make the current size the real scale of any selected object.

## Creating the background

For the background of the scene, we will need another 3D plane that will also receive a texture. But we can take a different approach from the logo image. Since the background image has a squared size of 400 x 400 pixels, we won't need to apply any changes to the scale.

Plus, it doesn't have any transparency requiring particular nodes in the **Shader Editor**.

Before we create the 3D plane that will receive the background texture, we can align the 3D cursor to make sure our object will appear in the center of the **3D View**. In Blender, you will always create objects using the 3D cursor location as a reference.

Go to the **View** menu and choose **Align View** | **Center Cursor** and **View All**, which will move the cursor to the center of your **3D View**.

Now, press the *Shift + A* keys and add a new plane. Press the middle mouse button, or the wheel and drag the mouse to orbit the scene. Use the blue arrow in the 3D plane to push the object backward. Make sure it will stay behind the text, as *Figure 5.12* shows:

Figure 5.12: Background plane location

Add a material to the 3D plane and open the **Shader Editor**, just like we did with the logo object. Change the material from **Principled BSDF** to **Diffuse BSDF** and, using the *Shift + A* keys, add the following nodes to the **Shader Editor**:

- **Input** | **Texture Coordinate**
- **Vector** | **Mapping**
- **Texture** | **Image Texture**

With all the nodes in place, use the **Open** button from the **Image Texture** and select the `spiration-light.png` file as the texture. In the **Mapping** node, you can change the **Scale** values to **3** on both the **X** and **Y** axis.

Connect all nodes, as *Figure 5.13* shows:

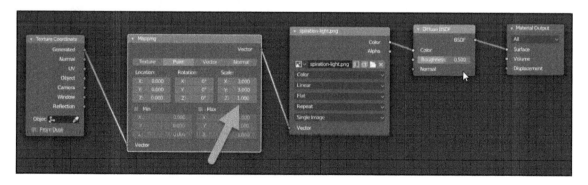

Figure 5.13: Connected nodes

Using the *S* key in the **3D View**, you can scale up the 3D plane until it fills the full background of your camera. Press the *0* key from the numeric keyboard to go back to camera view, and use the *S* key to make the adjustments. You should see the plane filling the space behind the camera (*Figure 5.14*):

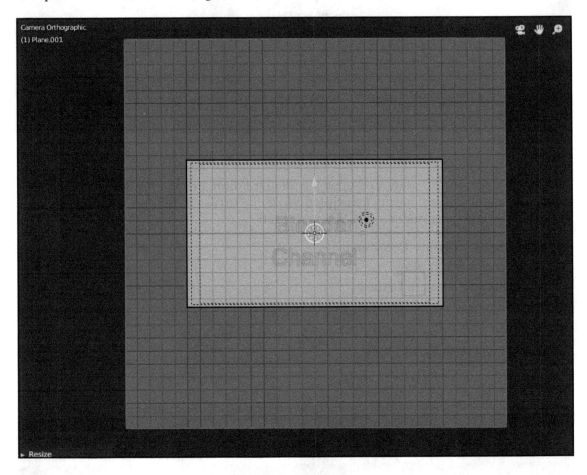

Figure 5.14: Plane behind the camera

# Creating animations for the intro

We have all the necessary graphics in place with textures, which gives us all we need to start making animations. The animation process here will work in a very similar way to what we did in Chapter 4, *Animated Properties for Video Effects*. You should add a keyframe to a property in at least two different moments in time.

From the difference between those keyframes, Blender will interpolate the intermediate values for that property to make an animation.

Here is a list of all animations we must create for the project:

- **Channel title**: Slide in the scene from the left and stop at the center
- **Logo**: Scale up from zero to the actual size
- **Background**: Slowly slide from left to right, to give a moving image in the back

The animation will be 5 seconds with a frame rate of 24. That means we need 120 frames. Open a **Timeline** window and set the **End frame** as 120.

# Animating the title

A technique used to facilitate animation production is to start adding keyframes at the end position of all objects. In cases where you have to build something like an intro video, it will give you the freedom to create all kinds of transitions for video.

With the timing for our intro set to 5 seconds, we can leave 1 second as reading time to leave all elements appearing on screen with no animations. That means everything must get to the final position by frame 96.

As a result, we can select the title text and move the playback head in the **Timeline** window to frame 96. Press the *I* key with the mouse cursor over the **3D View** window and choose **Location** to create a keyframe.

 You can also use the **Object** menu and the **Animation | Insert Keyframe...** option.

Now, go to frame 1, and using the red arrow from the **Text** selection, slide the object to the left until it stays outside the camera frame. Add another location keyframe with the *I* key.

If you hit the *Shift* + space keys, you will see an animation with the text sliding from left to right. The animation will look linear and not very appealing. We can improve it by adding a small extrapolation move.

What is an extrapolation move? To put it briefly, you should move the object a little further from the final point of motion, almost like it missed a stop.

Go to frame 90 and move the text to the right of the center. Add another location keyframe.

# Logo animation

For the logo, we will use a similar approach, but instead of going with a location animation, we can use scales. Follow the sequence of keyframe insertions for the respective frames:

- **Frame 50**: Since it will be the final state of our logo you don't have to make any transformations. Just press the *I* key and choose **Scaling**.
- **Frame 1**: Before adding the keyframe, press the *S* key. It will trigger a scale transformation. By pressing *0* and *Enter* on your keyboard, you will set the size to zero on all axes. Press the *I* key and add a scaling keyframe.
- **Frame 46**: For the extrapolation movement, we can press the *S* key again and type 1.3 on the keyboard followed by *Enter*. It will make the logo a lot bigger. Press the *I* key and add another scaling keyframe.

Notice how we started backward from frame 50.

# Background animation

The background plane will feature a much simpler animation, with a simple move from left to right. As a result, we won't need any extrapolation movement.

Here are the frames and actions required:

- **Frame 120**: Move the background to the left, until it almost reaches the right border of your camera. Press the *I* key and add a location keyframe.
- **Frame 1**: Slide the background to the opposite direction and make it get close to the left border of the camera frame. Press the *I* key to add another location keyframe.

# Animation timing and speed

At this point, you will notice that by pressing play to preview your animation, it will show the motion from all objects. However, you probably will want to make the title and logo move a little faster. In the current state, they are almost moving around in slow motion.

The best way to edit animation speed and timing is with the **Dope Sheet** window where we can individually change keyframe positioning.

Select the text with a right-click and, holding the *Shift* key, click to add the logo to the selection. Go to frame 1 in your **Timeline** window.

Change the window type from **Timeline** to **Dope Sheet** in the **Editor Type**. You will see a screen with both objects and their animation tracks. Each keyframe appears on that window a yellow diamond shape (*Figure 5.15*). Press the plus icon on the left of your **Dope Sheet** to display all animation channels:

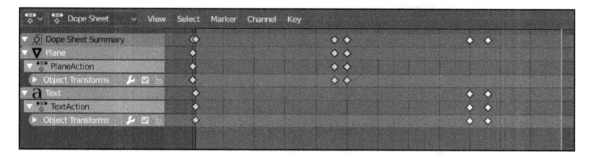

Figure 5.15: Dope Sheet window

With the frame set to position 1, any transformation in the keyframes will scale up or down with that frame as a pivot.

Press the *S* key with the mouse cursor on the **Dope Sheet** and scale down your keyframes, until the last diamond is at frame 20. If you want to select all keyframes, press the *A* key.

If you play the animation now, you will see much faster motion from both objects.

# Adding a scene to the Video Sequencer

Since we now have a full animation ready to use, we can go to the **Video Sequencer** Editor and add that introduction to any project we want. You have two main options to use such animations:

- Render the results as either video or image sequence
- Insert the intro as a scene to the **Video Sequencer**

Using the material as a scene will allow you to make changes to the text or graphics for different projects.

Before we add the scene to the Sequencer, we must rename the current scene to identify it in our Sequencer. At the top right of your screen, look for the scene name and set it as **Intro** (*Figure 5.16*):

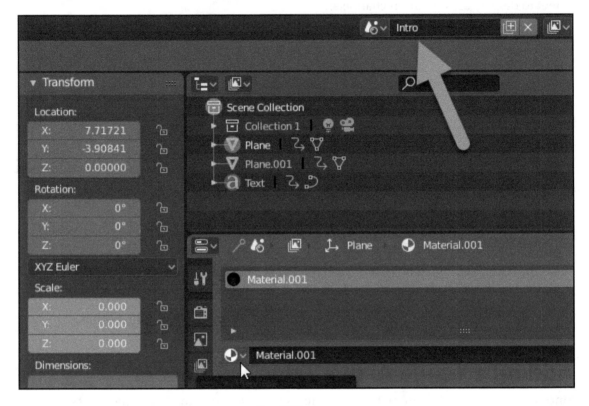

Figure 5.16: Scene name

Next, create a new blank scene by pressing the plus button right next to the box where we set the scene name. By the way, that box is also the scene selector. Choose **New** from the scene creation options.

Go to the **Video Sequencer** Editor, and in the **Add** menu, you will see our **Intro** in the **Scene** options (*Figure 5.17*):

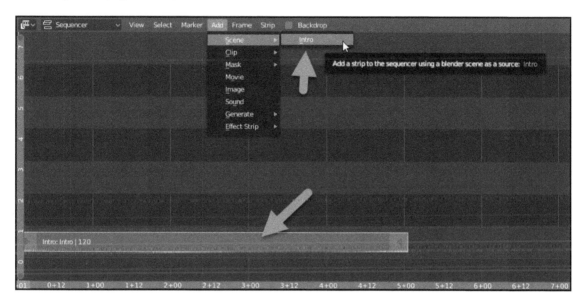

Figure 5.17: Scene selector

Once you add the scene to the Sequencer, you will get the total number of frames from that scene. You can add more footage following the intro to make a longer video!

Each scene can have a different animation duration. For instance, the Intro has 120 frames, and all new scenes will feature 250 frames. You can create multiple animations with individual lengths and blend them tighter using the **Video Sequencer**.

# Summary

Even though it is a simple example of how you can create an intro clip for a video in Blender, what you just learned will help you to develop many more animations for video. You have to add a few more textures, text, and 3D objects like the ones in the next chapter.

In the next chapter, you will see how to create 3D compositions from multiple tri-dimensional objects and how to add video to them as a texture.

# 6
# Using Videos as Textures for 3D Compositions

In Blender, you will find a wide range of tools and options to create animation for video, but it still lacks a few options for anything other than cutting pre-existing footage. What if you want to make a 3D composition with multiple objects and videos?

For that type of project, we have the option to use videos as textures. In this chapter, we will learn how to create a 3D composition using multiple objects and videos as textures. The technique will mimic a production environment you find in software such as Adobe After Effects.

Here is what you will learn:

- Using videos as textures
- Configuring playback of videos as textures
- Creating animation loops with videos
- Synchronizing multiple objects for animation

## Technical requirements

You will be required to have Blender 2.80 installed to follow this procedure. Even if you have a later version of Blender, the described example should work with no significant problems.

The media files of this chapter can be found on GitHub:
`https://github.com/PacktPublishing/Blender-for-Video-Production-Quick-Start-Guide/tree/master/Chapter06`
Check out the following video to see the procedures in action:
`http://bit.ly/2r9YteN`

# How to use videos as textures in Blender

The use of textures is an outstanding option in Blender to create rich graphics for any video production. When you mix 3D graphics such as planes with textures to make a video, you can create almost any type of content.

However, using textures will give you much more freedom to overcome a limitation of the **Video Sequencer Editor**. Until now, we have managed to add videos to the Sequencer to cut and mount in several different ways. One thing you can't do with videos in the Sequencer is to scale down two clips and show them at the same time in the render (*Figure 6.1*):

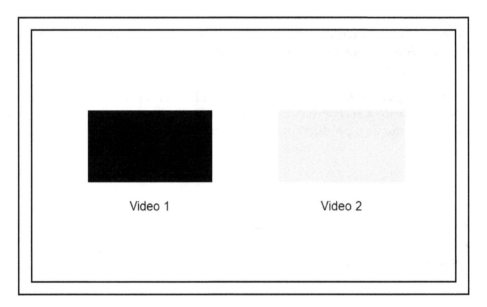

Figure 6.1: Two videos side by side

For projects that require you to create a more complex infographic using multiple videos at once, having this limitation will be a huge problem.

One feature of Blender related to textures will allow you to overcome that problem and successfully add multiple videos to the project. You can use videos as textures for objects in Blender.

Using that feature will give you the freedom to add as many objects and textures in a video as you wish.

# What types of textures can you use?

In Blender, you can use several types of video formats as textures. If you want to avoid any potential compatibility problems, I suggest the use of standard video files in containers, such as MP4 or MOV. For the codec, you should look for H264 for maximum compatibility and smaller sizes.

You can use other types of codec such as WebM or MPEG-4. As a rule of thumb, you can use the same formats that Blender can produce. Going in to the render options and the video settings will give you a list of all available formats and codecs.

# Using videos as textures

What do you need to use videos as textures in Blender? At this point, you already know how to use images as textures in Blender, and using videos will require only a small adjustment to the settings.

In the **Shader Editor**, you have the **Image Texture Node** that will give you an option to open the desired image file you need. At the bottom of your **Image Texture Node**, you will see the **Single Image** option as the default texture type. If you change that to **Movie**, you will be able to use a video file as a texture (*Figure 6.2*):

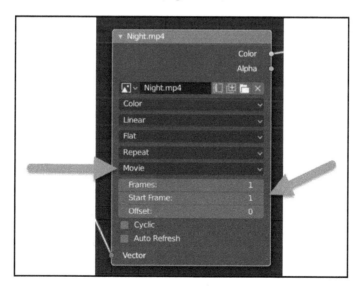

Figure 6.2: Image texture options

When you choose **Movie** in that node, you will see additional options:

- **Frames**: How many frames of your video file you wish to use?
- **Start Frame**: Pick a starting frame to display in your texture.
- **Offset**: You can offset the total amount of frames for your texture.
- **Cyclic**: Once Blender reaches the end of a video, it can start over from the beginning.
- **Auto Refresh**: Always mark this option to make Blender refresh the texture contents for video production on every frame.

That is all you need to use videos as textures in Blender.

# Composite 3D content with video

How do you use videos as textures in a practical project? To demonstrate how you can create the most visually appealing videos using such textures, we can create a small composite video made of a few 3D elements and video textures.

It will be an animated infographic describing popular travel destinations. It will look like *Figure 6.3*, which shows a vertical column on the left with the names of each destination, and two planes showing videos:

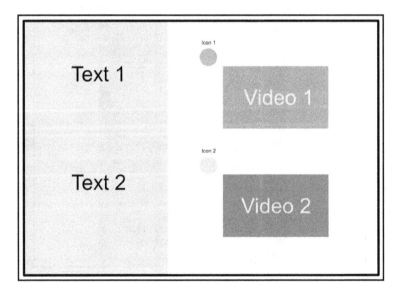

Figure 6.3: Project layout

As you can see from the image, we will have to create 3D elements such as planes like we did in the previous chapter.

# Creating the scene

The first step to doing our project is to create a new file in Blender, using either *Ctrl + N* or **File** | **New**. Pick the **General** option from the menu that will appear.

Erase the default Blender cube and set the camera in orthogonal mode, viewing the project from the top, exactly like we did in the previous chapter.

From that camera setup, we can start adding the visual elements of the scene. Using the *Shift + A* keys, create all the necessary text objects and set them with **Paris** and **Berlin** as text content.

 The method to align two 3D text objects in a project will require you to create the first text object. For the second text object, you can use a *Ctrl + D* to duplicate and move the new text in the Y-axis.

Place them on the left side of your screen and add a 3D plane in the background. If you rotate your viewing angle using the middle mouse button, the scene will look like *Figure 6.4*:

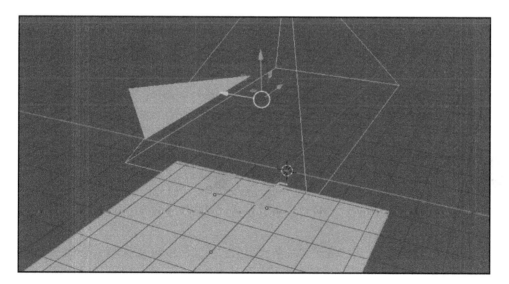

Figure 6.4: Scene layout with text

Next, we have to create the background plane that will stay behind both videos from our travel destinations. Add another 3D plane to the scene and, using both the *G* and *S* keys, make the necessary adjustments to scale it up to fill the area behind the camera.

Also, move the object to the back of your composition (*Figure 6.5*):

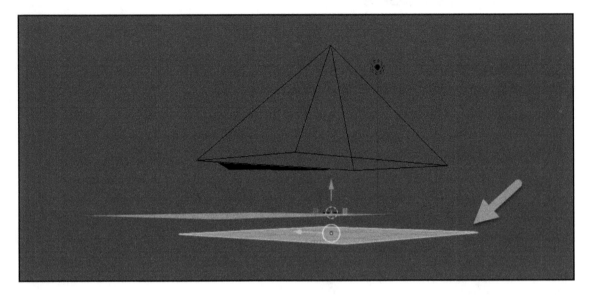

Figure 6.5: Backplane

The last objects we need for this project are all four planes that will receive textures. You need two small planes that will receive icon textures, and also the two large planes receiving our videos.

For those planes, you have to follow the same principle described in the previous chapter. You must set the object size to match the proportions of each texture. Both icons have a square format that will match the default size for any newly created plane in Blender.

However, our videos have a 16:9 aspect ratio. They have a 1920 x 1080 pixels resolution. After creating the first plane, change the dimensions of your object to 1.92 x 1.08 to match the video size. You need the right aspect ratio. Don't forget to press *Ctrl + A* and choose **Scale** to apply the transformation and duplicate the plane with *Ctrl + D*.

You should have the objects, as *Figure 6.6* demonstrates:

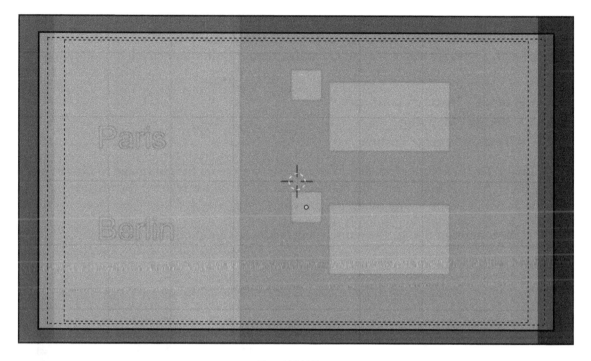

Figure 6.6: Initial layout

# Setting the project length

After you set the 3D plane dimensions in the properties sidebar, you can move on to set the length of the project. Our video will be 30 seconds in length, which means we need 30 seconds x 24 frames = 720 frames.

Go to the **Timeline** window and set the **End frame** as 720.

As for the videos we will use as textures, you must look for their durations. If they are less than 30 seconds in length, you must turn on the **Cyclic** option for the texture. Otherwise, the video will stop at the last frame.

If you have a video of more than 30 seconds in length, you might want to use the **Start Frame** of your video to pick a range that will give you the best visuals.

# Adding the textures to each 3D plane

It is now time to add the first texture in our plane. The process will require you to use the same material structure we used in the previous chapter. Select the object and add a new material with a **Diffuse BSDF** shader. Go to the **Shader Editor** and create the following nodes:

- **Input** | **Texture Coordinate**
- **Vector** | **Mapping**
- **Texture** | **Image Texture**

In the **Image Texture Node**, you should change the type from **Single Image** to **Movie**, and choose the video file. Make sure you mark **Cyclic** and **Auto Refresh** for the texture and pick the `paris.mp4` file or any other file you want.

Also, set the **Frames** option to `720` since it will be the full length of our project.

The final result of your material should look like *Figure 6.7*:

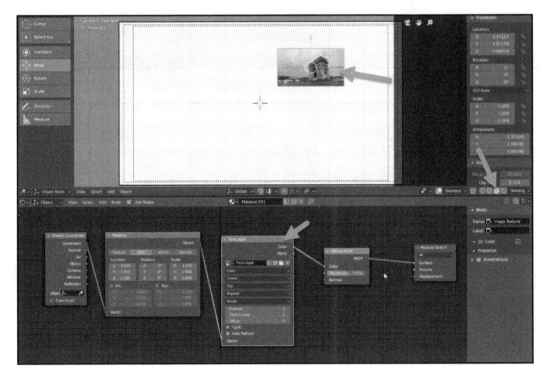

Figure 6.7: First video texture

Regarding the second texture, we can speed up the process of setting up the texture by making a copy of the existing material. Select the second 3D plane, and in the **Material** panel, you will see a selector for existing materials (*Figure 6.8*):

Figure 6.8: Material selector

Pick the material we used for the first plane. By the way, you can assign unique names for materials to make it easier to find them later.

Once you get the existing material, which in my case has a name of **Material.002**, you can duplicate the material by clicking on the plus icon next to the material name (*Figure 6.9*):

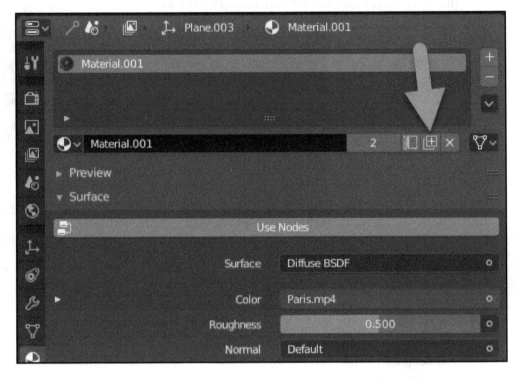

Figure 6.9: Plus button

You will see Blender adding a number to the end of your material name, and you now have a full copy of the first material. In the **Shader Editor**, you can change the video file in the **Image Texture Node**. Get the berlin.mp4 file, and we will have the material ready!

Still related to textures, you can add both texture icons to the upper and lower 3D planes.

# Previewing textures in videos

Unfortunately, Blender won't display your video textures in the preview window of the **Video Sequencer**. Is there a way to check if the video textures are working? To verify if you have working video textures, you will need to make a few test renders.

The technique is simple, and all you have to do is to choose a random frame and press *F12* to render a single frame of your animation. You will see a single frame of each video.

Now, pick another random frame and press *F12* again. Did you see a different frame from the videos? If the frames changed, it means you have working video textures.

One aspect of those videos that you can't preview unless you make a full test render producing a video is both speed and timing. For that, you can reduce the output size for something like 40% of the final result to speed up rendering.

# More materials and textures

For the rest of the objects in the scene, you can use the following approach. We will use solid colors for some of the objects and textures for the background plane behind both videos.

Here is how you should setup the materials and textures for each object:

1. **Plane behind two texts**: Apply a solid color. To get a great looking contrast, choose a light blue color.
2. **Text objects**: Since we want contrast, pick a plain white color for both.
3. **Small planes**: Apply the two icon textures for both objects. For those objects, I will use `traveler.png` and `airplane.png` for the upper and lower object.
4. **Background plane behind videos**: Apply a texture called `doodles.png` on the plane. Set the **Scale** to 3 on both the **X** and **Y** axis in the **Mapping Node**.

You should get all objects with textures and materials, as *Figure 6.10* shows:

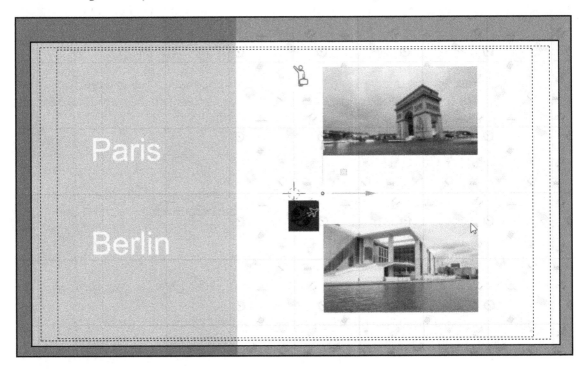

Figure 6.10: Scene with materials

# Animation and composition

What about the animation? To create the animation for this particular project, we will, once again, start from the last frame and build the rest of our motion. If you change your current frame to 600, you will have the final location for all elements in the infographic.

Select all objects in your scene, leaving only the camera and light source unselected. You can use the *A* key to select all objects, and right-click on the camera and light while holding the *Shift* key.

With the objects selected, use the *I* key to add a location keyframe for all of them.

# Animating the left panel

The left panel has a total of three objects: two instances of 3D texts and the background. Now, it is an excellent time to add some materials and colors for those elements. Make the text white and the background light blue for contrast.

All objects in this panel will enter the screen from the left. First, you will have the background sliding in until it fills one-third of the screen. When the background stops, you will have the first lot of text sliding in followed by the next.

Set your current frame as 48 and select the background plane. Add a location keyframe to the plane. Go to frame 1 and move the plane all the way to the left, until it is entirely out of the screen.

Press the *I* key and you can insert another location keyframe. Don't worry about timing at this point. We can adjust the speed of our animation later.

 If you choose to create animations for video using a different frame rate, remember to make the adjustments to the length. For instance, using 60 fps will require 1,800 frames for 30 seconds.

# Text animation

The text animation will follow a similar process with a different number of frames to sync and start moving. We will start getting the first text lot of moving after the background is in place. Since we set the final movement of that plane as frame 48, we will make both instances of text stay still from frame 1 to 48.

Keeping the backward technique, we are using until this point; you should start your process by marking the final location of the first text.

Here is a breakdown of each frame and the order in which you should edit them:

1. **Frame 60**: This will be the final text location, and since we already have it there, you can select the object and, using the *I* key, add a location keyframe.
2. **Frame 58**: Remember the extrapolation effect? Go to this frame and move the text just a little to the right, and add a location keyframe.
3. **Frame 48**: Move the text to the left, outside of your screen area. Add a location keyframe to the object.

From an animation perspective, the use of frame 58 is optional since it will only add the extrapolation effect. However, you should always use that type of extrapolation move to make the animation a lot more interesting.

What about the second instance of text? You can use the same frame distribution and actions, with a small adjustment. The second instance of text will start to move with a small delay.

Assuming the final frame, our second text is 70. You can add the keyframes in the following order:

- Frame 70
- Frame 68
- Frame 58

Use the same types of keyframes for those frames, and you will have the motion for the second text!

## Animating the right panel and videos

With our left panel ready, we can move on to finish animation at the right panel. The background plane will move from right to left in a simple slide motion. To synchronize this with all other pieces of the composition, you should use frame 80 as the final location, and 70 as the starting point:

1. **Frame 80**: Set the current frame to 80 and add a location keyframe. This will be the final location for our background.
2. **Frame 70**: Go back to frame 70 and move the background all the way to the right, until it is entirely out of the camera frame. Add a location keyframe.

By hitting *Shift* + space, you will see the background sliding into the scene from the right.

Now, it is time to work with our two planes that have a video texture. To keep our animations following the same pattern, we can use the same extrapolation technique. The first plane will have frame 90 as it's final location, and frame 100 will be the second plane.

Select the top 3D plane that has a video texture and in:

1. **Frame 90**: Add a location keyframe with the plane in their final location.
2. **Frame 88**: Move the plane just a little bit to the left, and add a location keyframe.
3. **Frame 78**: Move the plane all the way to the right, until it is out of your camera frame. Add a location keyframe.

That will set the animation for the camera. If you set the **Cyclic** option in your **Image Texture Node**, you will have an animation loop for the video. For the lower 3D plane, you can perform the same procedure, but with the following frames:

- Frame 100
- Frame 98
- Frame 88

As the last step is to set the animation for our project, we can add the motion for both icons in the project. The two objects will share the same starting and end frames, with the only difference being that one will slide in from the top and the other from below:

1. **Frame 120**: Select both objects and add a location keyframe. Don't move them around now, since frame 120 is their final location.
2. **Frame 118**: With only the top plane selected, move the object just a little towards the center. Add a location keyframe. Select the lower plane and repeat the process.
3. **Frame 110**: The final stage is to move objects outside of our camera frame. Get the top plane and move it up until it is out of the frame. Add a location keyframe. Repeat the process with the lower plane, but move it downwards instead. Add a location keyframe.

After all that keyframe and timeline manipulation, you will get a full working infographic. Have you noticed something interesting about the process we just performed? It is a repetitive task that will require you to add keyframes to multiple objects, working only about timing and the order in which things will move around.

That is a crucial point to create animations and infographics for video in Blender. It does not matter if you have only five or six objects to animate; you will probably use the same process for all objects.

# Adjusting timing for animations

Like all other projects that we made in previous chapters, you can change timing and motion using the **Dope Sheet** window. Although you can use the window to resize and set animation timing by spacing keyframes, you should take extra care with any edits.

Since we are using a synchronized motion for each element in our project, you should make group changes by selecting only a few objects at the time.

How do you do that? Open the **Dope Sheet** window and, using the selection tools in Blender, isolate just a few keyframes. For instance, you can use the *Alt+ A* key to remove all keyframes from a selection. And select only the objects you wish to adjust the animation for.

With the *B* key, you can draw a box around only a few keyframes you wish to edit, like the ones from the left panel (*Figure 6.11*):

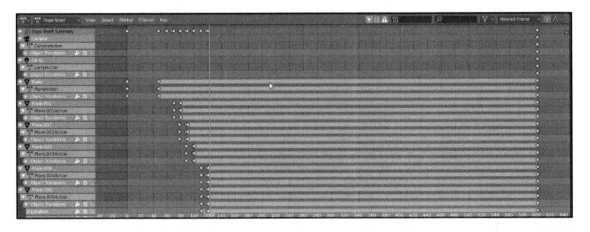

Figure 6.11: Dope Sheet keyframes

Once you have the keyframes selected, it is only a matter of choosing how to manipulate their timing. You can either use the *G* key to slide them backward or forward in time or, with the *S* key, change the spacing between each keyframe.

# Summary

At this point in the book, you already know how to edit and make animation projects for video, which will give you a wide range of options to create all sorts of videos. An animated infographic could help you make videos for advertising or education, or enrich an explanation of an idea.

But we still have something missing from the material! What would any material be that describes an idea without a voiceover?

In the next chapter, you will learn how to add and synchronize audio with your animation projects.

# 7
# Adding Sound and Voiceover for YouTube

What would any video project be without audio? Blender has a great set of tools for editing and producing video and audio. In this chapter, you will learn how to use those tools to cut, enhance, and manipulate sound in your projects.

You will learn that, using the same tools for video footage, we can also edit audio files. Audio files can include background music, effects, and also voiceover. No matter what type of media you choose, Blender will help you use it in your project.

Here is what you will learn:

- Importing audio to the Sequencer
- Editing and manipulating audio
- Syncing audio and video
- Protecting audio tracks already in sync
- Using effects for audio
- Applying animation to create dynamic effects

## Technical requirements

You will be required to have Blender 2.80 installed to follow this procedure. Even if you have a later version of Blender, the described example should work with no significant problems.

The media files of this chapter can be found on GitHub:
`https://github.com/PacktPublishing/Blender-for-Video-Production-Quick-Start-Guide/tree/master/Chapter07`
Check out the following video to see the procedures in action:
`http://bit.ly/2P9C8Yr`

# Using sound and voiceover for videos

One of the main benefits of using Blender to either edit or manipulate audio tracks is that you can use the same tools we already learnt about when working with video. The interface and tools will be the same. You don't need to learn anything new related to the Sequencer.

Of course, there are some differences in manipulating video data and audio, but we can quickly learn how to deal with that.

How do you get audio files in the Sequencer? Using the **Add** menu, you can get audio files such as MP3, OGG, or others in the Sequencer using the **Sound** option (*Figure 7.1*):

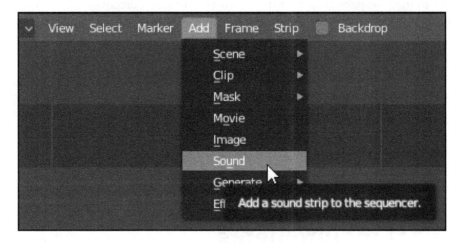

Figure 7.1: Add menu for sound

Once you add the audio track to the Sequencer, you will use the same shortcuts and options to edit and cut it. For instance, pressing the *K* key will trigger a soft cut on both audio or video strips.

By default, Blender won't show any visual differences between audio and video strips. You can turn on an option that will make each type of strip easier to identify. In the **View** menu, you have an option called **Waveform Displaying**. Choose **Waveforms On**, and you will see a visual representation of your audio files (*Figure 7.2*):

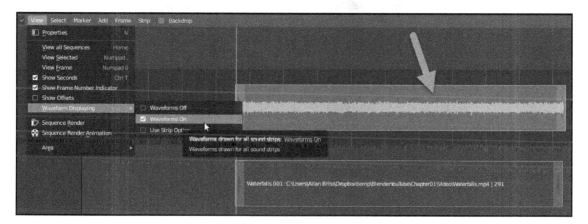

Figure 7.2: Waveform viewing

With the zoom controls, you can make the strips become taller and have a better view of your audio strips.

# Audio properties

Just like with video footage, you can also edit audio properties in Blender using the existing sidebar. When you select an audio strip, you will see the options to manipulate audio. The list of available properties to edit related to audio is much shorter than what we had for video.

You will find three properties, as *Figure 7.3* demonstrates:

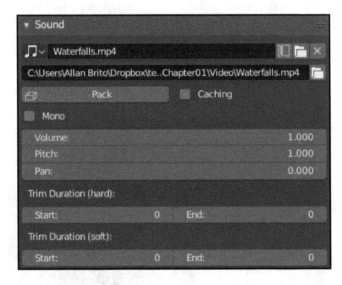

Figure 7.3: Audio properties

Here is what you can edit for audio:

- **Volume**: The name of this property is self-explanatory and will give us the ability to control how loud we will hear the audio. Using the default value of 1 means no changes will be made to the volume.
- **Pitch**: What is the pitch? Using this tool, you can change the perception of audio by manipulating the frequency. You can change someone's voice to make it thicker or feel sharper.
- **Pan**: For stereo tracks, you will be able to control how much of each audio will go for the left or right channels. The values range from -2 for left and +2 for the right channel.

Even with a short list of options related to audio properties, we can quickly fix an audio file that doesn't have the necessary volume level.

# Grouping multiple audio tracks with video

One aspect of working with audio and video in the Sequencer, with which you will want to take extra care, is their alignment. When you have two independent strips for audio and video, it might become critical to keep them in sync.

If you select any of the strips and press the *G* key, you can freely move them around, and once you do that, you no longer have audio and video in sync.

That will happen even for video footage that has an existing audio track. By selecting either one of them, just one, and pressing the *G* key will make you move the strip as a single object. As a result, you will get totally out-of-sync audio and video.

How do you avoid that? The solution to keeping your audio and video in sync is to create something called MetaStrips. Those strips will work as a group, preventing and keeping all footage in sync.

To create a **MetaStrip**, you have to select two or more strips and press the *Ctrl + G* keys. You will see a new visual for your footage and the name **MetaStrip** will display next to the object (*Figure 7.4*):

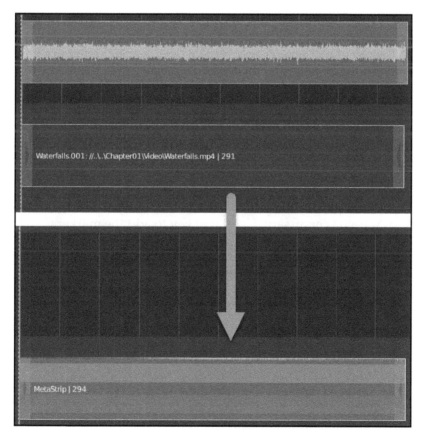

Figure 7.4: MetaStrips

The MetaStrips will lock access to the individual strips, which will prevent you from making any accidental changes to the footage. To view and edit the contents of a **MetaStrip**, you can press the *Tab* key with a MetaStrip selected.

And to split the contents of a **MetaStrip**, you can use the *Ctrl + Alt + G* keys. All options related to MetaStrips are also available in the **Strip** menu.

Use MetaStrips as a way to protect and lock content in the Sequencer for any media, and not only audio-related material.

# How to synchronize voiceover with video?

For projects that require you to use voiceover for video, you will need to find a way to align the voiceover and video content. In Blender, we have a perfect tool to allow for this alignment with the use of markers. Whenever you need a visual reference to set the position of footage in the Sequencer, you can add a marker with the *M* key (*Figure 7.5*).

How does a marker help with audio sync? By using markers in your projects, you can visually identify parts of a video that should match a speech.

For instance, assuming you are making a video review about a new smartphone model, and you want to start describing the product price, you have a voiceover for that particular video also discussing pricing.

To match and sync both parts, you can add a marker to the Start and End frames of your video where such speech is necessary. Use the *M* key to add the markers.

You can also use the *Ctrl + M* keys to rename each marker. Once you have the markers in place, you can get the voiceover strip and align that to the video (*Figure 7.5*):

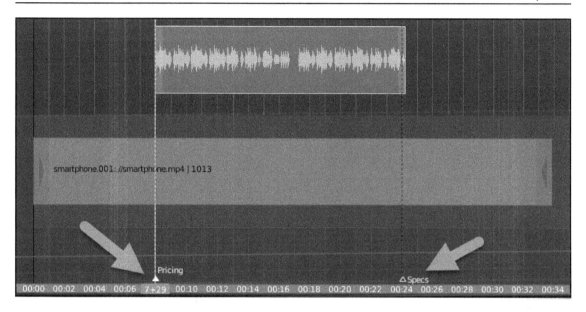

Figure 7.5: Markers for video

That is the easiest way to get voice and video in sync. If you use the **Sequencer preview** window to check and watch the results of your audio and video synchronization, an option may give you a significant boost in performance.

You can use the *K* key to make cuts to any audio strip.

Depending on your hardware, you may not see a real-time preview of your audio and video playback. But, if you reduce the **Proxy size** to something like 25%, it will improve playback performance.

To set the size of your preview proxy, you can use the sidebar located in the preview window. Use the + icon and open the sidebar. Set the **Proxy** size to 25%, and use the lowest possible quality (*Figure 7.6*):

Figure 7.6: Proxy size

You can set it back to **No proxy, full render** for the most extended quality preview.

# Effects for audio in Blender

Blender has a reasonable list of effects you can choose for video footage, which can help you enrich any project. But, when the subject is audio effects, the list will dramatically shrink.

If you take a close look at the **Effect Strip** list, you won't find any effect aimed at audio. What can we do with sound regarding effects?

For audio effects in Blender, we will have to use the properties in the sidebar. You can manage using volume controls and pitch. As for the effects, you will be able to see the property for the entire strip or choose only a small subset of your audio.

If you use the properties in the sidebar alongside keyframes, you will be able to apply those effects to only a small part of your audio strip.

Here is an example of how that will work. Assuming you have an audio strip that has 450 frames in duration, and between frames 300 and 390 you have a few words from the voiceover that need emphasis.

To get that effect, we will use the **Pitch** property to make the voice deeper between those frames.

Starting with frame 299, which is one frame before the beginning of our effect, you can add a keyframe to the property. While you have the mouse cursor above the **Pitch** property, press the *I* key.

In frame 300, change the **Pitch** value to 2 and add another keyframe. Go to frame 390 and add a keyframe.

As a way to set your effect only between those two frames, you can now go to frame 391 and return the **Pitch** to the default value. And add another keyframe.

The secret to creating effects in just a limited number of frames in any audio strip is the use of keyframes.

# Adding background music to a video

One of the most common effects you may want to use for a video is the creation of background music for the production. That will involve two audio tracks, where one of them is the voiceover; the other will be your background music.

The idea here is to make your background music start with a standard volume setting, and when the voiceover begins, you will lower the music volume to make it become just a faint sound.

How do you create such an effect? In Blender, you will make that effect by using the same procedure we already used in Chapter 3, *Using Properties to Enhance Video*.

Assuming you have a video that has your voiceover starting at frame 220 from a total of 885 frames, you can select the track representing the background music and set the current frame to 1.

In the sidebar, you will locate the **Volume** property for that audio, and add a keyframe. Place the mouse cursor on top of the value and press the *I* key. Go to frame 210 and also add a keyframe with no changes to the volume level.

At frame 220, set the volume value to 0.15 and add another keyframe. That will create a fade-out effect for your audio, which will help with the transition from full volume to a much lower level (*Figure 7.7*):

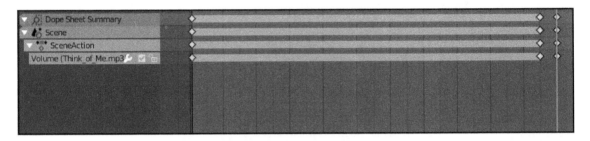

Figure 7.7: Keyframe distribution

After you set the keyframes for that property in your sidebar, you can get more visual control over the volume property.

In the video editing workspace, you can open a **Graph Editor**. With the audio strip still selected, you will see a curve representation of your keyframes (*Figure 7.8*):

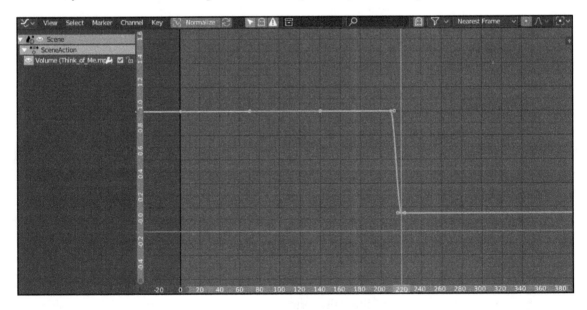

Figure 7.8: Graph Editor

Pressing the *Home* key will adjust your graph view to fit any window size you have. In the **Graph Editor**, you can right-click on each point in the graphic to move or adjust the effect.

For instance, if you feel your audio is way too low after frame 220, you can select the last keyframe with a right-click, and using the *G* key, move the point up. That will raise the volume of your background music.

The graphics view provided by this window will help you with interactive control over any animation data. By the way, you can use the controls on any other type of animation.

 You can control the curve transition for this graphic using the **Key | Handle Type**. Choose the **vector** type to have a linear transition or **smooth** for a gradual transition.

# Summary

Even with fewer options to edit and manipulate audio files in Blender, you can use the Sequencer to add that type of media to your projects. Using the effects and properties from the sidebar, you can change the nature of your audio to adapt the content to any project.

Blender even has an option to export audio-only projects, where you can use the Sequencer data to create podcasts and other types of media based on audio.

You will learn how to use those options in Chapter 9, *Exporting Video for YouTube*.

# 8
# Aligning 3D Content with Video Using Virtual Cameras

In some projects related to video production, you may want to use what we call a virtual camera, or track an object motion to replace it in a video later. That is quite common in productions dealing with some level of VFX.

Blender can perform some of those tasks with a powerful motion tracking system for video, which will allow you to use virtual cameras and track objects on the screen. In this chapter, you will learn how to use that system to add content to part of a video that was left blank while filming.

Here is what you will learn:

- How tracking works in Blender
- Using tracking marks to produce your videos
- Identifying the best points in a video for monitoring
- Adding markers to existing footage
- Processing tracking data
- Creating objects to follow tracking markers
- Composing a video with images or video using tracking data

# Technical requirements

You will be required to have Blender 2.80 installed to follow this procedure. Even if you have a later version of Blender, the described example should work with no significant problems.

The media files of this chapter can be found on GitHub:
`https://github.com/PacktPublishing/Blender-for-Video-Production-Quick-Start-Guide/tree/master/Chapter08`
Check out the following video to see the procedures in action:
`http://bit.ly/2RtnsFe`

# When to use virtual cameras and tracking

The use of Blender as a tool to produce video-related material is a great alternative when you need something like a non-linear video editor. As well as getting all the options regarding video editing, you also have at hand a full-featured 3D creation environment.

One of the advantages of that 3D environment is the ability to use motion tracking tools to make virtual cameras. The use of such motion tracking abilities will give you the power to work with all types of projects, blending live-action footage with virtual content.

A common use of such a technique is when you have footage with a green screen, and you want to add or replace content using that special space.

For instance, you may want to add a background to a scene or create something that is missing from the footage. For example, you can use this technique with technology videos, where you will get a device that doesn't have a system yet and add that later in a video.

In *Figure 8.1*, you will see a frame from a project that uses this concept; it shows an actor holding a smartphone that doesn't have a system on the screen. Instead of a full user interface, you will see a green screen with some markers:

Figure 8.1: Smartphone video

The green screen will help you replace all the colors from the video, but the real difference in that footage is the markers. There is a reason why the cross-hair is put in. Blender will search for interesting points in a video to create the virtual camera, and having points with high contrast will make the process of identifying those points a lot easier.

For that reason, if you need to produce such footage to later edit the content in Blender for tracking, you can add tracking points to any location. Just keep in mind that you will have to either hide or remove them from the final product.

# Using the Movie Clip Editor in Blender

The process to use and track video in Blender involves a special window that we haven't use until now. If you open the **Editor Type** selector, you will see in the list a window called **Movie Clip Editor** (*Figure 8.2*):

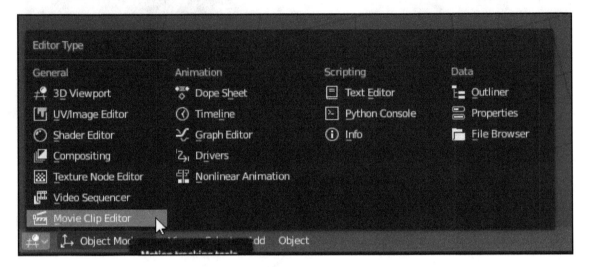

Figure 8.2: Movie Clip Editor

To get the most out of the features related to motion tracking in Blender, you can even used a special workspace. By clicking on the **+** to add a new workspace, you will see a section called **VFX** and an option called **Motion Tracking**.

By choosing this workspace, you will get the most important editors in Blender to perform tracking:

- **Movie Clip Editor | Clip View**
- **Movie Clip Editor | Graph view**
- **Movie Clip Editor | Dope Sheet view**
- **3D View**
- **Timeline**

Alongside the outliner and properties, you will be able to work and make virtual cameras and objects.

In the middle window, you will get the **Movie Clip Editor** with the **Clip View** enabled. Hit the **Open** button and find an MP4 file you wish to track. In our case, I will open the PhoneGreen.mp4 file (*Figure 8.3*):

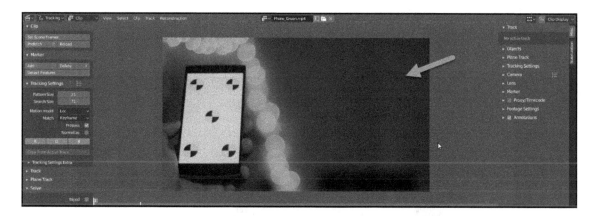

Figure 8.3: Video file in the editor

When you open a video file there, you will be able to control the playback with the **Timeline** options at the bottom of your screen.

# Tracking points in the video

How do we track points once we get a video in the **Movie Clip Editor**? To create tracking points for this particular footage, we have two options:

- Use the reference points in the middle of the screen
- Get the corners of the screen

The best solution is to use the screen corners because they offer a significant level of contrast. Inside the screen, we get a green color, and the phone body is almost black. It will be easy for the tracking points to follow the motion.

 If we went for the inside points, we would have to expand the points later to get the tracking plane aligned with the phone screen.

# Adding tracking points

The process of creating the tracking data needs something called **tracking markers**. You will need several of them to create useful tracking content. In this particular case, where we have a screen, you will need at least four markers.

Look to the left sidebar in your **Movie Clip Editor**, and you will find all the necessary options for managing tracking data (*Figure 8.4*):

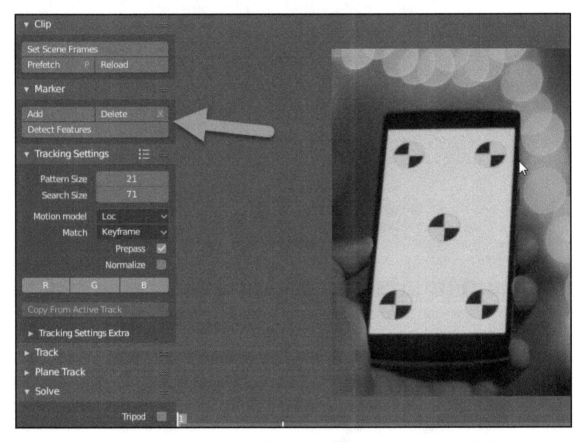

Figure 8.4: Tracking sidebar

Before you add any markers, make sure you have frame 1 as your current frame.

To add a marker, you can use the **Marker** section in the sidebar and choose **Add**. Once you hit the **Add** button, click anywhere in the video to create the small squared marker (*Figure 8.5*):

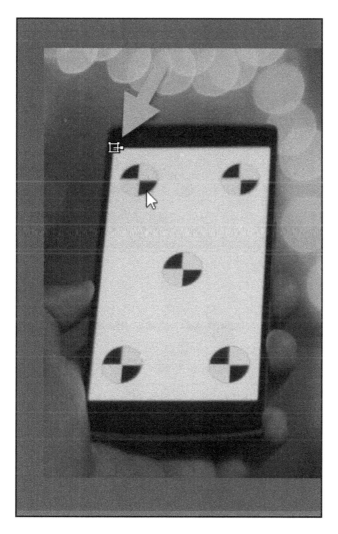

Figure 8.5: Tracking marker

You can click and drag the marker to a corner of the smartphone screen. Blender will even magnify the marker on the left to help you locate the marker in the best possible location (*Figure 8.6*):

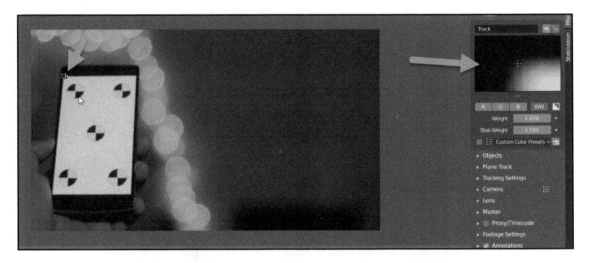

Figure 8.6: Tracking magnifier

You can use the same shortcuts to select and manipulate the markers that you use most often in Blender. Right-click to choose a marker and use the G key to move it.

On the right side of your marker, you will see a small line with a square in one of the sides. If you click and drag on that square, you will be able to scale up and down the marker size.

After adding the first marker, use the **Add** button to create another marker and make sure it is at another corner of the screen. Repeat the process two more times until you have four markers (*Figure 8.7*):

Figure 8.7: Tracking markers

We have the markers but no tracking whatsoever. If you play the video, there won't be any movement in the markers. To make Blender start tracking the video, you will use the **Track** options on the left sidebar.

There you will find a track section and controls. The play button will trigger continuous tracking from the current frame until the end. If you go to the next button, you will get single frame tracking. By using the buttons on the left, you will get the same behavior in the opposite direction (*Figure 8.8*):

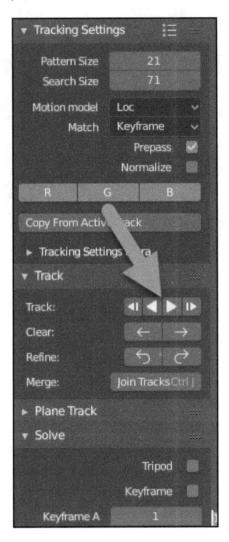

Figure 8.8: Tracking controls

Make sure the project is using the full length of your video before you start tracking. In our case, the video will end on frame 289.

Blender will only track the selected markers, and if you wish to follow all four of them, you must choose them all. Use the *A* key to quickly select all markers and hit the play button in the **Track** options. You will see the tracking graph showing that Blender is following motion in your video.

What if you don't like the results? You can increase the size of the marker and try again. You can erase tracking data from selected markers using the **Clear** option below the tracking controls. Set the current frame as 1 and use the arrow pointing right to erase all tracking data.

With the tracking data ready, you can hit the play button from the **Timeline**, and you will see all four markers following the screen.

# Using objects to track content

Having four markers following the screen in our video will give us the opportunity to create objects and align them with the markers. For instance, we can add a plane that has all four corners attached to each one of the markers.

Using the **Create Plane Track** on the left sidebar, you will add a plane to the video. Make sure you do that with the current frame set to 1 and all four markers selected. After you add the plane to the video, click and drag each corner until it aligns with a marker (*Figure 8.9*):

Figure 8.9: Plane Track

Try to cover all the area of the screen with the plane. Once you have the plane in place, just hit play to see it following all markers and deforming with them.

# Aligning content and rendering

Now we have got to the point where we can start rendering our project! However, if you press the *F12* key to render your motion tracking file, you will probably see only the default cube from Blender. Why is that? Unless you add something to the **3D View**, **Compositing**, or Sequencer, Blender doesn't know you want to render the video content.

For this particular project, we will use the **Compositing** editor to replace the tracking plane with either an image or a video.

Instead of changing the window type, we can start a new workspace. Press the + button and choose **VFX | Compositing**. You will see the **Compositing** editor (*Figure 8.10*):

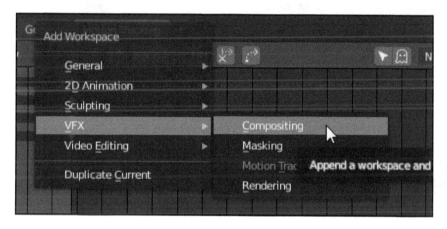

Figure 8.10: Compositing editor

To get started, we can turn on the **Use Nodes** and **Backdrop** at the top to enable nodes and see a preview of our video in the background, respectively.

It is time to add a few nodes in the **Compositing**, just like we did with materials. Erase the **Render Layers Node** and, using the *Shift + A* key, add the following:

- Input → **Movie Clip**
- Input → **Image**
- Distort → **Plane Track Deform**
- Converter → **Alpha Over**
- Output → **Viewer**

Connect the nodes, as shown in *Figure 8.11*:

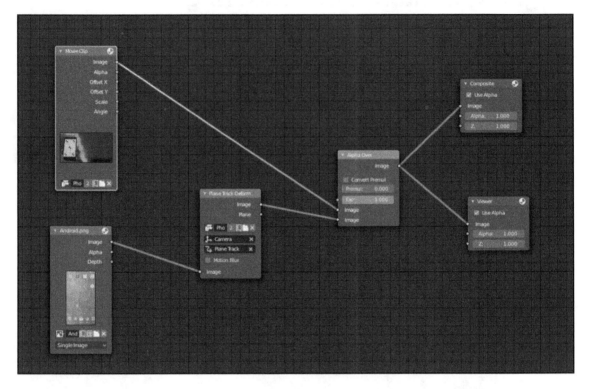

Figure 8.11: Nodes arrangement

In the **Movie Clip** node, you can select the video file we have opened and pick a texture for the **Image** node. I will use a screenshot from an Android phone, with the name of `Android.png`, which you can select using the small folder icon used to pick a file.

Using the **Plane Track Deform**, you have to select the virtual camera called **Camera** and the object called **Plane Track**.

 If you want to use another video instead of a still image, replace the **Image** node with another **Movie Clip** node.

What happens with this node layout? The node that blends both the video and image together is the **Alpha Over**. It gets the **Movie Clip Data** in the top input socket and the image deformed by the tracking data on the second socket.

Since we are using the **Alpha Over** for the mix, it will ensure that all pixels around the **Image** node are transparent, outside the actual image. Only the image will appear.

The **Viewer** node enables the preview in the background (*Figure 8.12*). You can use the *Alt + Home* keys to adjust the backdrop zoom:

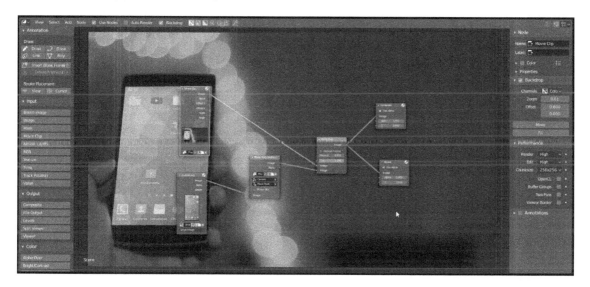

Figure 8.12: Render preview

If you hit play in the **Timeline**, a preview with all frames will appear in the **Compositing** background. Pressing *Ctrl + F12* will trigger the rendering of your video with the virtual camera.

Using that technique, you can add any image you want to the smartphone screen. It can be a full new design or even something like an iOS interface in an Android device.

To get a full description of how to render the project using either an image sequence or video, take a look at Chapter 9, *Exporting Video for YouTube*.

# Summary

The use of tracking for video is a great way to expand your video production ideas, and you can apply the same concept to replace other types of videos. For instance, you can change the facade of a building! All you need is to get the best possible tracking points to add a **Plane Track**.

Now that you know how to manage tracking data in Blender, the next step is learning how you can get that information and render it for production. Blender has an extensive list of options regarding rendering, and you will learn how to manage that in Chapter 9, *Exporting Video for YouTube*.

# Exporting Video for YouTube

# 9

The final stage of any project related to video production in Blender is the rendering. You may want to create an MP4, MKV, or MOV file from the contents of your Sequencer. But what are the best settings to get an optimal video for platforms such as YouTube?

In this chapter, you will learn how to set up Blender to render a project with all the recommended settings from YouTube itself, using the render properties. You will learn about:

- Choosing the proper render engine
- Setting up lights for intro animations and infographics
- Using the render settings in Blender
- Choosing and creating video presets
- Preparing a project with the best settings for YouTube
- Organizing the project with image sequences

## Technical requirements

You will be required to have Blender 2.80 installed to follow this procedure. Even if you have a later version of Blender, the described example should work with no significant problems.

Check out the following video to see the procedures in action:
http://bit.ly/2zvndTk

# Preparing a project for exporting and rendering

Getting to the stage where you are ready to render a project is always exciting because you are close to seeing that big project come to life. However, before you jump into rendering a project, you must do a few things before pressing the *Ctrl + F12* shortcut for rendering.

The first task is to ensure we are using the correct renderer. Blender will give you two main options for rendering:

- **Eevee**
- **Cycles**

In the **Render** tab of the **Properties** window, you can choose between them and set up your project rendering. Nowadays, **Eevee** is the most exciting option for rendering in Blender because it is capable of making real-time graphics. But it is still in development and doesn't support some basic features we need, such as transparent PNG files, as textures in the **3D View**.

For that reason, you should choose **Cycles** to render any project related to the use of transparent textures in PNG.

 The renderer will make a difference when you have material from the **3D View** that needs rendering. For footage in the Sequencer only related to video or audio, you won't get any notable difference from either **Cycles** or **Eevee**.

# Lights and environment settings

Besides choosing the renderer of your project, you might want to get the lights in the right layout. If you try to render some of the animations we create in the book, you will notice something weird. They will look dark and have too many shadows.

Blender is 3D software and will interpret a scene as if you were about to make a 3D animation.

We must remove the lights and set a uniform and constant illumination. To achieve those settings, you must erase all lights in the scene. After that, you can open the **World** tab in the **Properties** window (*Figure 9.1*):

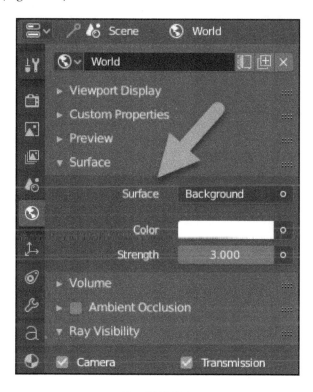

Figure 9.1: World tab

In that tab, you will look for the **Surface** options. If you see the **Use Nodes** button, that means you need to activate nodes first. Press that button to see all options related to the **World** settings. There you will be able to pick a color for the background.

In both **Cycles** and **Eevee**, the background will add light to the scene. By choosing a white background, you will get a full bright light casting over all objects with the same intensity. Having no lights also means no shadows.

Look at an example scene using only a background plane and 3D text (*Figure 9.2*):

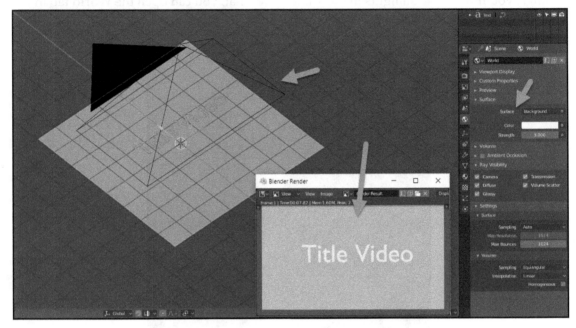

Figure 9.2: Render example

If you raise the **Strength** option, you will get a brighter light in the scene and more vivid colors.

# Exporting settings for video

To export a project for YouTube, we have to follow some specific guidelines provided by the support area of the site itself. If you want to check the best possible settings for uploading video, you can visit `https://support.google.com/youtube/answer/1722171?hl=en`.

After visiting the page and looking for the specifications, you will see some critical aspects to render a video project such as:

- **File container**: MP4
- **Video codec**: H264
- **Audio codec**: AAC
- **Bitrate**: Will depend on resolution and frame rate

There are other settings for video, but those are the most critical aspects of a video that you will find in the Blender user interface.

Where are these options? You will find the render output options in the **Properties** window in a tab called **Render output** (*Figure 9.3*):

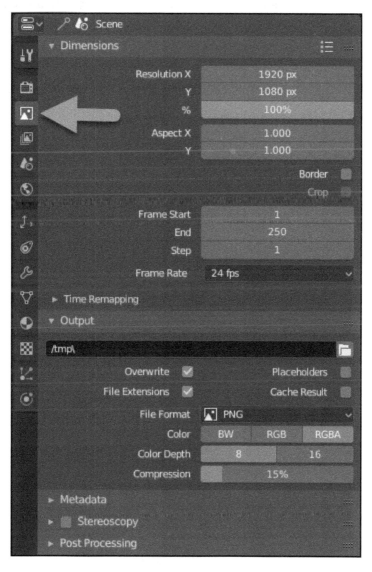

Figure 9.3: Render output

Before we proceed, it is important to point out a critical setting. We will use **Cycles** options for all rendered output. Remember to set **Cycles** as the default engine in the **Render** options.

Once you open the options, you will see at the top the dimension options where you can pick the resolution and frame rate. By default, Blender will start with a resolution of 1920 x 1080 pixels, which is also known as 1080p. Below the resolution, you can apply a scale factor to that resolution.

For instance, if you want to make a quick test render, set the scale to 25% and the output size will shrink down to only a quarter of the size.

There you will also find the frame rate settings, which is 24 by default.

What if you want to use something else, such as a 4K video? At the top of your panel, you can use presets for lots of video standards (*Figure 9.4*):

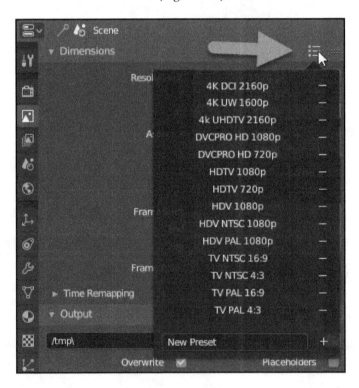

Figure 9.4: Video standards presets

If you pick the preset for **4K UHDTV 2160p** video, you will get a resolution of 3840 x 2160 pixels. For other video formats that are not present in the list, you can always use the **New Preset** option in that same list. Type the name of your preset and press the plus icon.

Blender will use the current resolution you have for the new preset.

 Notice that with the preset options, you can only change the resolution and all other settings will require manual configuration; including the frame rate for your video.

# Optimal settings for YouTube

The best way to explain how to export videos with optional settings for YouTube is with a practical example. In the recommended settings on the YouTube support page, you will find a list of characteristics for an optimized video for the platform in the 1080p format with 30fps:

- **Container**: MP4
- **Video codec**: H264
- **Audio codec**: AAC
- **Video bitrate**: 10 Mbps
- **Audio bitrate**: 384 Kbps

Where can you set all those options? First, change the frame rate in the **Property** field for the render output.

In the **Output** field, you will find an option called **File Format**. It will show **PNG** as the default option. Change from **PNG** to **FFmpeg** video (*Figure 9.5*):

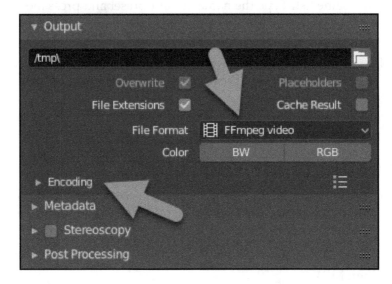

Figure 9.5: Choosing video output

By the time you choose **FFmpeg** as the output, you will see a new set of options called **Encoding**. That is the place where you will select all the important settings for the video output.

 Notice that YouTube recommends unique settings for each resolution of the video. The difference between settings will appear when you change the frame rate. You will have to increase the bitrate when using higher frame rates.

In that panel, you have to perform adjustments in seven places (*Figure 9.6*):

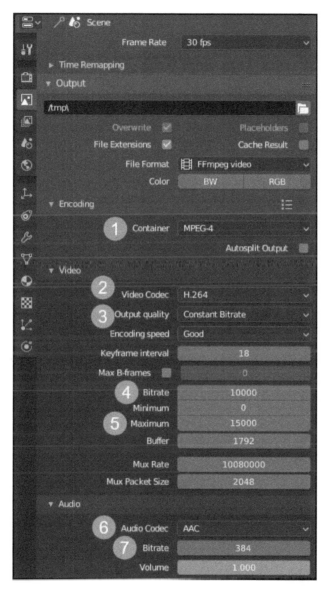

Figure 9.6: YouTube settings

Based on what *Figure 9.6* shows, you can do the following:

1. **Container**: Choose **MPEG-4.**
2. **Video Codec**: Get the **H.264** from the list.
3. **Output quality**: If you don't change this to **Constant bitrate,** you won't be able to choose the bitrate. Instead, Blender will offer options such as **High quality** or **Low quality** to render the project. This will produce good results, but you won't have full control over the bitrate.
4. **Bitrate**: Blender uses kb/s for the bitrate, and YouTube recommends 10 Mbps. Set the value as 10.000 kb/s.
5. **Maximum**: You will choose here the top value Blender can use for video exporting. For this parameter, you can use the current bitrate plus 50% to give the exporter plenty of room to use more demanding scenes.
6. **Audio Codec**: Choose **AAC.**
7. **Bitrate**: In the audio section, set the bitrate to 384.

If you use all those settings with footage in the Sequencer, you will get an MP4 file optimized for YouTube. Where will Blender save that MP4 file?

You can choose the folder where Blender will save the file at the top of your **Output** settings. In *Figure 9.5*, you can see the option right at the top.

 Blender will always use the footage in the Sequencer for rendering unless you disable the **Sequencer** option in the **Post-processing** field.

By pressing *Ctrl + F12* or using the **Render** menu and the **Render Animation** option, you will trigger the rendering process.

# Exporting audio-only projects

What if you want to export the audio from a Sequencer project? To get only the audio from a project, you can set the **Video Codec** option to **No Video** and make Blender skip all video data. In the **Audio** settings, you can pick an audio codec that you like.

For instance, you can choose MP3 as the codec for your audio (*Figure 9.7*):

Figure 9.7: Audio only project

Use the same *Ctrl + F12* and the **Render Animation** to export the audio.

# Using image sequences to organize the project

When you get a project in the Sequencer with all the necessary strips and audio, you can start to think about rendering to create an MP4 file. But instead of getting all the data from a project and rendering straight to video, you may want to get it as an image sequence first.

The reason to use image sequences in Blender for video is that it might save you some time and work as a backup. For projects that require multiple parts such as an intro and several scenes, you can start making image sequences whenever possible.

If your project doesn't require immediate use of audio, you can always render image sequences first.

We can use as an example the intro created in `Chapter 5`, *Creating Intro Videos for YouTube Text and Motion Graphics*. You can export that animation as an image sequence, and add the audio later.

Having the animation as a sequence of images will bring the following benefits:

- **Backup**: You will protect the render from potential crashes. When you render hundreds of frames, and your computer crashes in the middle of the process, you can pick it up from the last frame. Rendering a video would require you to start from scratch.
- **File compression and quality**: Using a sequence of PNG files will get you the best possible image quality with lossless compression. You can render the image sequence again to output multiple combinations of compression and keep all original image files.
- **Speed**: When rendering from an image sequence, you will notice that your computer will process the project with high speed. It is only processing images now.

How do you create image sequences? Just pick PNG as the output format and choose a folder. Blender will render the Sequencer results as a series of images in that same folder.

Later, you can add the images to the Sequencer by using the **Add** | **Image** option and choosing all images with the *A* key.

Use the video output as an MP4 only for the final project where all the assets and footage are in place. For the shorter parts, you can use image sequences for optimization purposes.

# Summary

At this point, you have all the necessary knowledge to start a video-related project in Blender. You can grab the footage from either your camera or smartphone and add titles, effects, and sound.

From that footage, you can create all types of projects and upload for your YouTube channel or any other platform related to a video.

# Other Books You May Enjoy

If you enjoyed this book, you may be interested in these other books by Packt:

**Blender Cycles: Materials and Textures Cookbook - Third Edition**
Enrico Valenza
ISBN: 978-1-78439-993-1

- Create a basic Cycles material by mixing the shader components
- Connect nodes of different kinds to build more advanced materials
- Add node-based textures to the shaders
- Create both simple and complex materials following step-by-step recipes
- Switch the shader components easily without affecting a possibly complex network of links
- Parent and rename the nodes to better organize the Node Editor window
- Build material interfaces for general use in complex materials by grouping the shaders inside groups
- Set up light sources and world global illumination

## Blender 3D Printing by Example
Vicky Somma
ISBN: 978-1-78839-054-5

- Using standard shapes and making custom shapes with Bezier Curves
- Working with the Boolean, Mirror, and Array Modifiers
- Practicing Mesh Modeling tools such as Loop Cut and Slide and Extrude
- Streamlining work with Proportional Editing and Snap During Transform
- Creating Organic Shapes with the Subdivision Surface Modifier
- Adding Color with Materials and UV Maps
- Troubleshooting and Repairing 3D Models
- Checking your finished model for 3D printability

# Leave a review - let other readers know what you think

Please share your thoughts on this book with others by leaving a review on the site that you bought it from. If you purchased the book from Amazon, please leave us an honest review on this book's Amazon page. This is vital so that other potential readers can see and use your unbiased opinion to make purchasing decisions, we can understand what our customers think about our products, and our authors can see your feedback on the title that they have worked with Packt to create. It will only take a few minutes of your time, but is valuable to other potential customers, our authors, and Packt. Thank you!

# Index

adding 136, 138, 140, 141
in video 135
transparency animations
making 62, 65, 66
types, data compression
lossless compression 17
lossy compression 17

# V

video container compatibility 16
video footage
frame rate, matching 14, 16
importing, to Blender 12, 14
Video Sequencer
about 7
scene, adding to 97, 99
time code, adjusting 17, 18, 19
zoom, adjusting 17, 18, 19
video strips
properties, in Blender 42, 43
selection 20, 21
transforming 21, 23
video, editing for YouTube
preview range, using 35
project length, adjusting 33, 34
video
animating 114, 115
background music, adding 127, 129
composite 3D content, using with 104
cropping 48
cut tools, using 28, 30
editing, for YouTube in Blender 28
editing, with markers 31, 32, 33

flipping 50
offsetting 48
opacity 45, 46
reversing 49
scene, creating 105, 106
settings, exporting for 150, 152
Snap, using for 37, 38
sound, using for 120, 121
textures 111
textures, adding to 3D plane 108, 109
textures, previewing 110
tracking points 135
used, for grouping audio tracks 122
used, for grouping multiple audio tracks 124
using, as texture in Blender 102
using, as textures 103, 104
visibility 45, 46
voiceover, synchronizing 124, 126
voiceover, using for 120, 121
workspace 10, 12
virtual cameras
using 132, 133
voiceover
synchronizing, with video 124, 126

# W

workspaces 7

# Y

YouTube
intro, creating for 80
optimal settings 153, 156
workspace 10, 12

www.ingramcontent.com/pod-product-compliance
Lightning Source LLC
Chambersburg PA
CBHW080532060326
40690CB00022B/5097